DEATH AND TAXES

DEATH AND TAXES

Some Perspectives on Inheritance, Inequality, and Progressive Taxation

Richard E. Wagner

American Enterprise Institute for Public Policy Research
Washington, D. C.

Richard E. Wagner is a senior research associate with the Urban Institute. The views expressed in this monograph are those of the author, and should not be interpreted as reflecting the views of the Urban Institute or its sponsors.

ISBN 0-8447-3100-5

Domestic Affairs Study 13, May 1973

Library of Congress Catalog Card No. L. C. 73-81113

Printed in the United States of America

ACKNOWLEDGMENTS

My preparation of this monograph has been aided by valuable counsel from several people. While I was preparing the first draft during the spring of 1971, Professor Jacques Melitz, then of Tulane University and now of the French Ministry of Finance, was a continual source of stimulating insight into basic issues concerning the role of inheritance in a free society. My approach to inheritance and the taxation of wealth transfers has been influenced considerably by our many discussions. During the fall of 1972 I received many helpful comments on a later version of this monograph from Martin J. Bailey of the University of Rochester and the U.S. Office of Tax Analysis, James M. Buchanan of Virginia Polytechnic Institute and State University, Harold M. Hochman of the Urban Institute, William A. Niskanen of the University of California, Berkeley, and Jacob A. Stockfish of the Rand Corporation.

CONTENTS

INTRODUCTION

The levy of a tax upon the occasion of a person's death has become a hallowed tradition of American fiscal practice. In 1825 Pennsylvania levied an inheritance tax of 2.5 percent on collateral heirs, thereby becoming the first state to tax wealth transferred at death. All states but Nevada now impose some form of tax upon such transfers of wealth. A federal inheritance tax was enacted, and later repealed, in the Stamp Act of 1797; subsequently such a tax was temporarily imposed during the Civil War and again during the Spanish-American War. It was not until the Revenue Act of 1916, however, that death taxation became a permanent fixture in the federal tax arsenal.

The federal government's system of transfer taxation has remained essentially unchanged for a generation. The present rate and bracket structure was adopted in 1941, and the only subsequent change of significance—the marital deduction—was introduced in 1948.

Interest in the performance of our system of transfer taxation has been growing steadily in recent years. During the past decade both the American Law Institute and the Brookings Institution sponsored major studies of our estate and gift taxes. These projects were followed on 5 February 1969 by the Treasury's proposals for substantial reform of our system of transfer taxation. And in a speech before the State Bank Division of the American Bankers Association on 12 October 1970, Wilbur D. Mills, chairman of the House Ways and Means Committee, said that reform of the estate and gift tax system stood high on his committee's agenda. Although recent developments have postponed such consideration, substantial interest nonetheless seems to exist concerning possible revision of Sections 20 and 25 of the Internal Revenue Code of 1954.

This volume explores several issues relating to transfer taxation. I shall try especially to place transfer tax reform into some perspective with regard to the larger issues of taxation and public expenditure. A particular tax institution may be examined within two distinct perspectives, and this monograph examines transfer taxation from both perspectives. One perspective views the prevailing format of separate tax provisions for wealth transfers as given and examines issues of reform within that context. If we assume that separate tax provisions for wealth transfers will remain in force, it is important to examine such issues as the choice of a rate structure, the selection of the unit of taxation, the response to trusts, the scope of gift taxation, and the treatment of concurrent taxation by federal and state governments. In a second, contrasting perspective, I consider the entire tax system as variable. Since transfer taxation is but one possible element of a tax system, the primary issue within this perspective is whether transfer taxation should continue as an independent form of taxation, or whether transfers of wealth should be treated as income under a considerably reformed personal income tax.

The analysis will shift intermittently between these two perspectives, at times examining the possible place of transfer taxation within the larger system of taxation, and at other times examining particular aspects of transfer taxation. Chapter 1 describes the essential purposes of a system of taxation and examines the possible scope for transfer taxation within this system. Chapter 2 analyzes the relation between progressive taxation, particularly transfer taxation, and inequality in the distribution of wealth and income. Chapters 3 and 4 examine particular aspects of transfer taxation: Chapter 3 considers some of the primary economic effects and Chapter 4 discusses some important, technical issues. Chapter 5 concludes by summarizing the implications of the preceding analysis for transfer tax reform. (The prevailing structure of transfer taxation is described in an appendix.)

1
TRANSFER TAXATION AND THE TAX SYSTEM

Since transfer taxation is but one element of our tax system, its role cannot meaningfully be discussed without first having some idea of the social function of a tax system. A tax system performs two primary functions: it raises revenue to finance the supply of public services and, in conjunction with public expenditures, it transfers wealth among individual citizens.[1] Transfer taxation must be evaluated, therefore, on the basis of its performance in both of these roles.

Transfer Taxation to Raise Revenue

The first of the two primary functions of a system of taxation is to raise revenue to finance the supply of public services. Publicly provided services, like parks, police, and education, differ from privately provided services in that, for the most part, they are not packaged and sold to individual consumers. Rather, such services are made freely available to all, with the services being financed by taxes levied upon the citizenry. A tax, then, is a political substitute for a market price.

The allocative performance of a system of taxation in financing public services depends primarily on how closely the tax institution establishes individual tax prices that approximate the prices that would be established by a private market. If the demand for public

---

[1] Richard A. Musgrave, *The Theory of Public Finance* (New York: McGraw-Hill, 1959), pp. 3-27. Musgrave lists three functions but recent research has made it questionable whether the third function—to stabilize the economy through variations in taxes and expenditures—can in fact be performed. See, for instance, Milton Friedman and David Meiselman, "The Relative Stability of Monetary Velocity and the Investment Multiplier in the United States, 1897-1958," in Commission on Money and Credit, *Stabilization Policies* (Englewood Cliffs, N. J.: Prentice-Hall, 1963), pp. 165-268.

services should rise proportionately with income, a system of proportional income taxation will approximate the results that would have emerged under a system of market pricing.[2] The selection of a tax institution, then, can clearly exert an important influence on the efficiency with which budgetary choices are made. Whenever services are not packaged and sold to individual consumers, the knowledge provided by market transactions regarding demand and cost is lost. Demand is instead reflected through a budgetary process, in which some tax institutions are more adequate proxies for market pricing than others. Hence it is important to consider the probable relation between the base of a tax and the demand for the service it finances.

A primary virtue of income taxation is that the demand for many public services varies more or less directly with income. Whether a tax system that substitutes perfectly for market pricing would be proportional or progressive, and if progressive, how progressive, depends upon the relation between the change in demand with respect to income and the change in tax liability with respect to income. At a very general level, and with numerous exceptions, however, a system of income taxation is a way of approximating the prices individual citizens would pay for those services if such services were packaged for sale on the market.

Are there reasonable grounds for suggesting that a tax on wealth or net worth could either substitute for income taxation or complement it?[3] If this question is answered "yes," we must then ask whether we can look upon taxation of wealth transferred at death as a convenient substitute for an annual tax on net worth. In principle, of course, a wealth tax is indistinguishable from an income tax, for any income flow can be assigned an equivalent capital value. If an asset yields an annual income of $10,000, and if the rate of return on capital (the interest rate) is 10 percent, the capital value of the asset will be $100,000. An annual tax of 10 percent on the income is then identical to an annual tax of 1 percent on the capital value. Since a capital value is simply a present discounted value of a future income stream, income taxation at t percent would be equivalent to capital taxation at tr percent, where r is the rate of interest. This identity of income and capital taxation suggests that only one of the two bases should be used.

[2] For an elaboration of this point and a specification of the necessary caveats, see James M. Buchanan, "Fiscal Institutions and Efficiency in Collective Outlay," *American Economic Review*, Proceedings, vol. 54 (May 1964), pp. 227-35.

[3] For a "yes" answer, see Alan A. Tait, *The Taxation of Personal Wealth* (Urbana, Ill.: University of Illinois Press, 1967), pp. 19-21.

In practice, however, the base of a capital tax differs from that of an income tax. Under the personal income tax, the cost of maintaining physical capital is an expense that is deductible in computing the net taxable income from that asset. Human beings, however, are not allowed to deduct the cost of maintaining their human capital in determining their tax liability. This pair of observations prompts the argument that the income tax discriminates against human capital relative to physical capital, and encourages the suggestion that a net worth tax should be adopted to create an offsetting discrimination against physical capital. If this line of argument were correct, the adoption of a net worth tax to complement the income tax would be a means both for restoring equity between human and nonhuman sources of wealth and for promoting an efficient allocation of resources between human and nonhuman forms of wealth.[4]

An annual net worth tax would require an annual assessment of such personal assets as real estate, consumer durables, stocks, bonds, bank deposits, and cash. The capricious administration of personal property taxes is widely acknowledged, and it is far easier to value real estate than personal property or intangible assets. Thus an annual net worth would involve several times the administrative difficulties of a personal property tax. Faced with these realities of tax administration, a tax levied upon the estate of a decedent may be viewed as a convenient substitute for an annual net worth tax. If wealth accumulation typically begins at age forty and death takes place at seventy, one valuation of wealth upon death would replace thirty during a decedent's life.

---

[4] An "earned" income exemption from the personal income tax could accomplish much the same effect without requiring the development of a new form of tax.

The argument that the personal income tax discriminates against human capital is strongest when individuals must pay for their own investment in human capital. Much investment in human capital is subsidized, of course, which reduces the discrimination against human capital. It is possible, as I illustrate below, for the amount of subsidy to become large enough even to reverse the direction of discrimination. Consider two initial investments of $100,000, one in human capital and one in physical capital. Suppose the annual gross return is $20,000 in both cases, and that annual maintenance costs are $5,000. Let the rate of tax on taxable income be 50 percent. Taxable income from physical capital is $15,000, thus the post-tax rate of return is 7.5 percent. Taxable income on human capital is $20,000, which gives a post-tax rate of return of 5 percent. The impact of "free" education can be illustrated by assuming that the human capital is acquired with a personal outlay of only, say, $50,000. The $5,000 post-tax income from human capital now represents a rate of return to the recipient of 10 percent. Thus the combination of personal income taxation and the heavy subsidization of human capital formation discriminates against physical capital, not human capital.

Given the amount of tax actually extracted from a decedent's estate, a series of annual taxes could always be designed that could have extracted the same present value.[5] If we assume, for arithmetic simplicity, that the interest rate is zero, a death tax of $30,000 would be equivalent to an annual series of thirty net wealth taxes of $1,000 each. Recognition that interest rates are positive complicates the arithmetic without disturbing the principle of equivalence being illustrated. The exact impact depends upon whether we take as a base a $30,000 payment upon death or thirty annual payments of $1,000 during life. If equivalence is defined in terms of a $30,000 payment upon death, the annual taxes would be some amount less than $1,000 such that the actual payments plus accumulated interest sum to $30,000. If equivalence is defined in terms of thirty annual payments of $1,000, the levy upon death would exceed $30,000 by the sum of the accumulated interest earned by the annual payments.

Death taxation may thus serve as a substitute for net worth taxation. The United Kingdom has made substantial use of the estate tax as a source of revenue, and raising revenue is probably the dominant objective of the British estate tax.[6] In 1954, for instance, 15 percent of British deaths resulted in liability for estate taxation.[7] The comparable figure for the United States at that time was one percent. The specific exemption in the United Kingdom is only $7,200, compared with $60,000 in the United States. Although the maximum rates are nearly the same, 80 percent in the United Kingdom and 77 percent in the United States, the highest British rate begins at $2,400,000 while the highest American rate begins at $10,000,000. The British and American estate taxes tend toward the same burden above $10,000,000, but the tax burden on small and medium amounts of wealth is much larger in the United Kingdom than in the United States.

Death taxation once a generation, however, is a poor substitute for wealth taxation once a year. An annual net worth tax would take as its base approximately the entire stock of nonhuman wealth in

---

[5] Tibor Barna, "The Burden of Death Duties in Terms of an Annual Tax," *Review of Economic Studies*, vol. 9 (November 1941), pp. 28-39. Nicholas Kaldor, "The Income Burden of Capital Taxes," *Review of Economic Studies*, vol. 9 (Summer 1942), pp. 138-57. A. C. Pigou, *A Study in Public Finance*, 3rd ed. (London: Macmillan and Co., 1942), pp. 138-46.

[6] "The main object of the tax [the British estate tax] has always been the raising of revenue. . . ." G. S. A. Wheatcroft, "The Anti-Avoidance Provisions of the Law of Estate Duty in the United Kingdom," *National Tax Journal*, vol. 10 (March 1957), p. 48.

[7] Ibid.

the economy. But only a small share of the nation's stock of wealth will ever change hands through death. The preponderance of personally owned wealth is consumed before death. Much wealth, for instance, represents savings made during the middle years of life which will be consumed by the owners during their retirement. If people followed perfectly such a life cycle pattern of saving, they would spend their last cent the instant before death, and die penniless. Under this extreme set of circumstances, none of the economy's capital stock would change hands upon death and death taxation could not substitute at all for net worth taxation. Since people do pass wealth at death, though only a fraction of what they once possessed, death taxation can be looked upon as a substitute for net worth taxation, though a relatively poor one.[8] Since death taxation is a poor substitute for net worth taxation, it cannot be viewed as a reasonable institution for financing the supply of public services.

Transfer Taxation to Redistribute Income

A second function of a system of taxation is to alter the distribution of wealth and income among individual citizens. A shift from a proportional income tax to a progressive income tax of equal yield alters the structure of tax payments made by the citizenry, increasing the payments made by those in the upper income ranges and reducing those made in the lower ranges. Since transfer taxation cannot be viewed primarily as an instrument for financing the supply of public services, it should perhaps be viewed primarily as an instrument for altering the distribution of wealth and income. The limited revenue yield,[9] the high level of the specific exemption, and the steeply progressive rate schedules all suggest that our system of transfer taxation is designed primarily to penalize the ownership of large amounts of wealth per se. To the extent that transfer taxation succeeds in preventing the accumulation of large fortunes, moreover, the revenue

---

[8] Local property taxation is a far closer approximation to a net worth tax on nonhuman wealth.

[9] Estimated federal estate and gift taxation collections for fiscal 1972 were $5.3 billion, of which $1.5 billion was nonrecurring revenue due to a one-shot speed up on the timing of tax collections. The sustainable revenue yield of $3.8 billion is less than 2 percent of estimated federal budget receipts. See *Budget of the United States Government, 1972* (Washington: U.S. Government Printing Office, 1971), pp. 73-74. State governments collected about $900 million from their death and gift taxes in fiscal 1968, which also is less than 2 percent of their total revenue. See *Facts and Figures on Government Finance*, 15th ed. (New York: Tax Foundation, Inc., 1969), p. 175.

yield from transfer taxation will fall. This conflict between the revenue and the "social" objectives of transfer taxation is analogous to the conflict between a protective tariff and a revenue tariff: A perfectly protective tariff will yield no revenue, and a tariff that generates the maximum revenue will yield little protection.[10]

Acceptance of transfer taxation to accomplish "social" objectives is doubtless aided by the widely held attitude that the acquisition of wealth by inheritance is less laudatory than the acquisition of wealth by personal effort.[11] The belief is strong, moreover, though it is not supported by the available evidence, as we shall see in Chapter 2, that wealth begets wealth and poverty begets poverty. It is often alleged that a tendency toward cumulative inequality characterizes a free enterprise economy, with rich people coming from wealthy families and people from poor families caught in a vicious cycle of poverty. Since inherited wealth is viewed by many as both a significant source of inequality and, more significantly, as tending to produce a cumulative inequality in the distribution of wealth, transfer taxation has perhaps understandably been supported as an instrument to help mitigate these tendencies.

Since transfer taxes fall upon prosperous decedents and their successors, albeit unequally among such persons, transfer taxation can be regarded as a crude means of taxing large fortunes. A policy designed to promote the negative objective of penalizing the ownership of large wealth should not be equated, however, with a policy designed to promote the positive objective of greater equality of opportunity in trying to gain wealth. The total value of personally owned wealth in the United States exceeds $2 trillion, so transfer taxes transfer annually only about 0.2 percent of the amount of wealth held by individuals. Moreover, the tax collections contribute to the general support of the government budget, only a small share of which contributes directly to promoting greater equality of opportunity. Since transfer taxation penalizes the ownership of large amounts of wealth, in a purely arithmetical sense a relative advantage is given to those who do not own large amounts of wealth. But the penalty is small and the benefits are diffused among the populace, so the con-

[10] Vasco N. P. Fortuna, "The Sociometric Theory and the Estate Duty," *Public Finance*, vol. 6, no. 3 (1951), pp. 267-71, shows clearly the inherent conflict between the revenue and the social objectives of death taxation. Fortuna specifically notes that if the social objective were fully attained, death tax revenues would fall to zero. (Fortuna, incidentally, argues that estate taxation should be used wholly to reduce inequality in the distribution of wealth.)

[11] Alan A. Tait, "The Taxation of Wealth at Death: A New Proposal," *Scottish Journal of Political Economy*, vol. 9 (February 1962), p. 40.

tribution of transfer taxation to the positive goal of equality of opportunity is negligible. Like many criminal sanctions, transfer taxation might appropriately be regarded as penalizing one segment of the population without significantly assisting the remainder. Transfer taxation, then, should not be viewed as an instrument for promoting some equalization of opportunity by preventing tendencies toward cumulative inequality.

From one perspective, then, it hardly seems sensible to have transfer taxation as an element of a tax system, for there are more appropriate instruments available both for financing the supply of public services and for transferring income among individual citizens. At several points in this volume, especially in Chapter 5, I shall inquire as to what form of tax system would perform more effectively than a system containing separate transfer taxes.

From another perspective tax institutions take on lives of their own, and modification of a tax while maintaining the basic structural framework is far more likely than the replacement of prevailing tax institutions. Since our transfer tax institutions are far more likely to be modified than to be repealed, much of the remainder of this volume—especially Chapters 3 and 4—is devoted to examining issues regarding reform of prevailing transfer tax institutions. Since mild reform is far more likely than radical transformation, I give considerable attention to issues of reform. Yet radical transformation seems likely to be superior, and the politically infeasible ideas of today become the political agenda of tomorrow, so I also devote considerable attention to issues relating to such radical transformation.

2
TRANSFER TAXATION, PROGRESSIVITY, AND THE CONCENTRATION OF WEALTH

It seems clear that transfer taxation exists primarily to penalize the accumulation of large amounts of wealth. And, as a matter of arithmetic, the penalty must reduce somewhat the inequality in the distribution of wealth. Transfer taxation, however, cannot be viewed seriously as an instrument to reduce inequality or to promote greater equality of economic opportunity, for other tax instruments would perform far more effectively in this respect. Transfer taxation penalizes some of the wealthy without significantly assisting the nonwealthy, and in some respects may even penalize the nonwealthy as well.

A Static Perspective on Inequality

Few topics seem capable of stirring emotions so violently as the inequality in the distribution of income and wealth. The basic facts concerning inequality ostensibly are quite simple. The lowest fifth of families in terms of income earn just over 5 percent of the income earned by all families, and the second-lowest fifth of families earn just over 12 percent. The highest fifth of families, by contrast, earn about 42 percent and the second-highest fifth earn nearly 24 percent.

It is widely recognized, however, that figures on the distribution of income overstate the extent of inequality, for such figures result from merging sets of individuals that should be kept separate while interpreting the figures. The relation between age and income is but one example, and can serve to illustrate the issues involved in interpreting the figures. A person's lifetime income profile typically starts low, rises until it peaks during the middle years, then falls off during the retirement years. Consider a world in which all people have identical lifetime income profiles. Figures on the distribution of income will show substantial inequality, with the exact amount depending upon the relative numbers of people in each age class and the rate at which income rises and falls over a person's life cycle. Yet the community should properly be regarded as one of perfect equality in the distribution of income, as all persons will earn equal incomes over their lifetimes.

It is also widely recognized that nonpecuniary differences among occupations will cause the statistics on the distribution of income to overstate the extent of inequality. Other things equal, if people prefer to live in less populous rather than more populous areas at equal wage rates, they will live in more populous areas only if they are compensated by a higher wage. Such factors as this also produce inequality in the distribution of money income, but this inequality in monetary forms of income is necessary to offset an opposing inequality in nonmonetary forms of income. Much inequality in the distribution of income is precisely of this nature. Generally, the higher the educational requirements for entering an occupation, the higher the annual income in that occupation. But at least part of this higher annual income is necessary merely to offset the higher costs of entering that occupation, both the monetary costs of education and the income that could have been earned during the years of schooling. Once again, statistics on the inequality of incomes exaggerate the actual amount of inequality.

Moreover, figures on the inequality of incomes by themselves provide no basis for judging the performance of an economy. Without some notion of an optimal or most preferred degree of inequality, there is no basis for saying that more equality or less equality is desirable. While admonitions to increase the degree of progressivity in our tax system are pervasive, and have been stimulated by the resurgence of populist rhetoric, advocates of such measures rarely specify the point at which such measures would cease—in other words, the desired degree of inequality.

Perhaps the most prominent attempt to specify an optimal degree of inequality is Abba P. Lerner's argument that the optimal degree of inequality is zero.[1] Ignoring possible disincentive effects of complete equalization, perhaps the most damaging argument against

[1] Abba P. Lerner, *The Economics of Control* (New York: Macmillan Co., 1944), pp. 26-32. For more recent efforts, see Ray C. Fair, "The Optimal Distribution of Income," *Quarterly Journal of Economics*, vol. 85 (November 1971), pp. 551-79; and Lester C. Thurow, "The Income Distribution as a Pure Public Good," *Quarterly Journal of Economics*, vol. 85 (May 1971), pp. 327-36.

perfect equality as an ideal is that it is an ideal under which few people would want to live. With rare exception, people prefer to take a chance at earning an above-average income even though this implies they may end up with a below-average income. For instance, in an experiment I performed at Tulane University between 1968 and 1972, nearly 400 students were faced with the necessity of choosing among alternative distributions of income.[2] While three students indicated they preferred an equal distribution of income, the remainder preferred to participate under conditions where the distribution of income was unequal. A few preferred extreme degrees of inequality and a few preferred only slight inequality, but most preferred distributions of income that approximated the prevailing distribution of income in the United States. The most preferred distribution of income was characterized by a guaranteed minimum reward of about one-third the average reward, and above this minimum base the amount of inequality roughly resembled the current distribution of income. This evidence would seem to suggest that, aside from the very bottom of the income scale, there is probably little wrong with the prevailing distribution of income. Or perhaps it merely suggests that the distribution of income is not really the object of concern after all.

A Dynamic Perspective on Inequality [3]

The statistical form of the distribution of income may have considerably less importance than the rate of mobility within the distribution, especially among generations. To illustrate, consider three individuals with incomes of $12,000, $8,000, and $4,000. Let us posit that the shape of this distribution will remain unchanged as time passes. One extreme possibility is that a child will come to occupy the same income position as his parents. Thus, children of parents with $12,000 will always have $12,000, and so forth. The other extreme possibility is that a child's income position will be wholly

---

[2] I determined the total number of points to be awarded on any single exam, the total number of exams for the semester, and the relation between total points and the course grade. The relation between points and grade was set such that the mean point value would yield a C+ grade, which was approximately the mean grade for the entire university. Each student faced the task of indicating his preferred distribution of the total points for an examination among the individual exams: that is, they had to specify the number of points to be given to the exam that I ranked first, second, and so on.

[3] For an elaboration on many of the points raised in this section, and also in the remainder of this chapter, see Richard E. Wagner, *The Public Economy* (Chicago: Markham Publishing Co., 1973), pp. 155-65.

Table 1

MEDIAN INCOME OF FATHERS AND SONS
BY FATHER'S OCCUPATIONAL CLASS, 1960

Father's Occupation	Father's Median Income	Son's Median Income
Managers, officials, and proprietors	$6,664	$5,747
Professional, technical, and kindred	6,619	5,737
Craftsmen, foremen, and kindred	5,240	5,195
Sales	4,937	5,608
Clerical and kindred	4,785	5,504
Operatives and kindred	4,299	4,834
Service, including private household	3,310	4,833
Laborers, except farm and mine	2,948	4,686
Farmers and farm managers	2,169	4,234
Farm laborers and foremen	1,066	4,021

Source: Lowell E. Gallaway, "On the Importance of 'Picking One's Parents'," *Quarterly Review of Economics and Business*, vol. 6 (Summer 1966), p. 12.

unrelated to his parents' income position. Thus, children of parents with $12,000 will have an equal chance of earning $12,000, $8,000, or $4,000. In either of these two extreme cases, however, the degree of inequality in the distribution of income will be identical. Although the distribution of income is identical in these two extreme cases, these cases would hardly be considered identical. This suggests that the focus of concern is not the amount of inequality in the distribution of income, but the rate of mobility within the income scale. If one-half the population received $5,000 and one-half received $10,000, the distribution of income would be considerably more equal than the current distribution. Yet without mobility among the two income positions, about one-half the populace would probably reject the prevailing social order.

A substantial amount of mobility seems to exist within the American distribution of income and wealth. In his study of income mobility over time, Lowell E. Gallaway found that 77 percent of the difference between the average income in the United States in 1960 and the median income of the lowest income class was eradicated within one generation.[4] Table 1 shows that the occupational classification with the lowest income in 1960 was "farm laborers and foremen," which had a median income of $1,066. The median income of sons whose fathers belonged to this occupational class, however,

[4] Lowell E. Gallaway, "On the Importance of 'Picking One's Parents'," *Quarterly Review of Economics and Business*, vol. 6 (Summer 1966), pp. 7-15.

Table 2

MEAN I.Q. OF PARENT AND CHILD BY PARENT'S OCCUPATIONAL CLASS

Parent's Class	Mean I.Q. Parent	Mean I.Q. Child
Higher professional	139.7	120.8
Lower professional	130.6	114.7
Clerical	115.9	107.8
Semi-skilled	97.8	98.9
Unskilled	84.9	92.6
Average	100.0	100.0

Source: James E. Meade, *Efficiency, Equality, and the Ownership of Property* (London: Allen & Unwin, 1964), p. 50.

was $4,021. Thus, 77 percent of the gap between their fathers' incomes and the average incomes of all fathers of $4,907 was eliminated by mobility within the income distribution. The opposite effect occurred at the top of the occupational scale. The median income of "managers, officials, and proprietors" in 1960 was $6,664. But the median income of sons from this class was only $5,747. Table 1 shows clearly that sons from the upper classes tend to earn above-average income while sons from the lower classes tend to earn below-average incomes. But Table 1 also shows that the income of sons from the upper classes tends to fall toward the average income while the income of sons from the lower classes tends to rise toward the average income.

The evidence indicates that individual incomes have a tendency to regress toward the mean. While people in the upper income class are likely to find their relative position worsening over time, people in the lower income classes are likely to find their relative income position improving. This tendency for income to regress toward the mean seems attributable to two factors. On the one hand, random elements pervade all economic activities, so luck has much to do with one's economic fortunes.[5] On the other hand, biological inheritance, primarily intelligence, places constraints upon the options that one is likely to be able to exploit.[6]

[5] Recall that ancient piece of Hebrew wisdom: "Speed does not win the race nor strength the battle. Bread does not belong to the wise, nor wealth to the intelligent, nor success to the skillful; time and chance govern all." Eccles. 9:11 (New English Bible).

[6] Biological inheritance may itself be viewed as a matter of luck, as the outcome of a genetical poker game.

It is well established that intelligence regresses toward the mean. While children of parents with above-average IQs will tend to have above-average IQs, their IQs will tend to be less than those of their parents. Similarly, children of parents with below-average IQs will tend to have below-average IQs, but their IQs will also tend to exceed those of their parents. Table 2 illustrates this regression toward the mean for six occupational classes. While the mean IQ of parents in the higher professional class was 139.7, the mean IQ of their children was only 120.8. And while the mean IQ of parents in the unskilled class was 84.9, the mean IQ of their children was 92.6. From generation to generation, there is mobility within the intelligence scale, even though the inequality in the distribution of intelligence remains constant. Thus, to the extent that high intelligence produces high income, biological inheritance will produce an intergenerational regression toward the mean income.

Luck also plays a strong role in the distribution of income from year to year. One's personal efforts by themselves play only a modest role in determining one's income. True, one may be able to increase his income by working longer hours or by undertaking special training, though even these opportunities must have somehow availed themselves in the first place. But perhaps the most significant changes in the income prospects facing people stem from changes in circumstances that are largely beyond their control. The value of a college education was oversold in the aftermath of the post-Sputnik hysteria, and the preponderance of college graduates now find it difficult to find jobs commensurate with their expectations, due largely to changes in external circumstances.

Any decision by an entrepreneur to create a new product or by an individual to train himself for a certain occupation is in part a gamble. In all cases an expected rate of return may be computed based on current circumstances. But future conditions will almost certainly differ from present conditions, and some people will gain by the discrepancy and some will lose. For example, people who decided a decade or two ago to become areospace engineers faced bright income prospects that unforeseeably have since turned bleak. Or consider an industrial worker working for a firm that experiences a strong increase in demand for its output, and as a result of the additional labor that is hired, finds himself promoted to foreman. Such an improvement in income prospects is also wholly a matter of chance.

Some people will have a run of good luck in that they invest in areas that will undergo unforeseeable increases in the relative demands for their output. Others will have a run of bad luck in that they invest in areas that will suffer relative decreases in demand. There is a considerable, largely unappreciated, amount of random variation in the distribution of income. The contemporary mythology that the wealthy get wealthier and the poor get poorer is truly a myth. If anything, the wealthy get poorer and the poor get wealthier.

A person with a relatively high income is likely to be one who has benefitted, among other things, from a run of good luck. Similarly, a person with a relatively low income is likely to be one who has suffered a run of bad luck. But luck tends to even out over time. A person may flip a coin ten times and receive all heads. But if he continues playing, tails will appear. Persons with large incomes and wealth will often find their run of good luck turning sour if they continue playing. It is not at all uncommon for relatively wealthy persons to lose their fortunes and even file for bankruptcy, indicating the equalizing power of luck. Similarly, the person who has been dealt a series of bad hands in a poker game will get some good hands if he continues playing. Income and wealth positions are continuously changing. There is no such thing as a cumulative inequality of income and wealth. In fact, the opposite may be descriptively more accurate, as regression toward the mean seems to characterize the distribution of income and wealth. Wealth may grow, but it can also decay, and the greater the wealth, the more compelling the forces of decay.

Inequality and Confiscatory Taxation

Assertions about the cumulative inequality of wealth are usually derived from a line of argument based upon the arithmetic of compound interest. And the arithmetic of growth at compound interest is truly inexorable. If a capital sum grows at 5 percent compounded annually for thirty years, the terminal value will be 4.32 times the initial value. Under these circumstances, it would take an average rate of tax on estates of 77 percent to prevent the accumulation of wealth from generation to generation. Five percent per year is a very modest rate of return once one allows for inflation. Yet if $1,000 had been invested 200 years ago at 5 percent compounded annually, the present capital value would be $17,298,000. If $1,000 had been invested 200 years ago at 10 percent, which is about the average return on common stock, the present capital value would be $189,670,000,000. If wealth grew under these conditions, any ten families that had $1,000 each 200 years ago would together now own practically all of our stock of privately owned wealth (about $2 trillion).

Although reasoning about wealth based upon compound interest is tempting because of its simplicity, it is also contradicted by the evidence. Fortunes do not accumulate at the average rate of return of the economy. Rather some birth and death process is operating. Fortunes may grow for a while, but either incompetence or bad luck will ensure their eventual death. A highly competent person will tend to be plagued by biology with less competent heirs. Moreover, a run of bad luck eventually will strike even the most competent person.[7]

The problem of "the gambler's ruin" is perhaps the most fruitful way of examining the distribution of wealth over time. In its simplest form, the problem of the gambler's ruin states that the probability that a gambler will lose his fortune varies inversely with the size of his fortune relative to that of his opposition. If the gambler, whose fortune is X, and his opposition, whose fortune is Y, face equal likelihoods of winning, the probability that the gambler will eventually lose his entire fortune is $1 - X/(X+Y)$. If the gambler and his opposition are equally rich, 0.5 is the probability of the gambler's eventual ruin.[8]

Especially relevant is the case of the infinitely rich adversary. As the wealth of the adversary increases relative to that of the gambler, the probability of the gambler's eventual ruin approaches certainty. In an economic system, the individual is playing against everyone else, so the individual trying to amass wealth is in the position of a gambler playing against an infinitely wealthy adversary. Although the gambler may encounter lengthy strings of good luck, he will eventually encounter a string of bad luck that will dissipate his fortune.

Of even greater interest than the probability that any given fortune will become exhausted is the expected length of time it will take to exhaust the fortune. It is relatively uninteresting by itself to argue that any fortune will become ruined, for it might take 50 years or it might take 500 years. The expected length of time it will take for the gambler to become ruined is of critical importance, if only 50 years the result may be a happy one, but 500 years may be intolerably slow.

---

[7] On these points see George J. Stigler, *The Theory of Price*, 3rd ed. (New York: Macmillan Co., 1966), pp. 307-09.

[8] The problem of the gambler's ruin is surveyed in William Feller, *An Introduction to Probability Theory and its Applications*, vol. 1, 2nd ed. (New York: John Wiley and Sons, Inc., 1957), pp. 311-13.

Table 3

PROBABILITY OF AND EXPECTED DURATION BEFORE GAMBLER'S RUIN

Probability of:		**Initial Fortunes of:**		**Probability of Gambler's Ruin**	**Expected Number of Plays Until Ruin**
Gambler's winning (p)	Gambler's losing (q)	Gambler (X)	Opposition (Y)	(P_r)	(D_r)
0.5	0.5	10	90	0.9	900
0.4	0.6	10	90	1.0*	50*
0.33	0.67	10	90	1.0*	30*
0.5	0.5	10	990	0.99	9900
0.4	0.6	10	990	1.0*	50*
0.33	0.67	10	990	1.0*	30*

* These values are extremely close approximations. The exact entry for P_r in the second row is 0.999999. Similarly, the exact value for D_r in the second row is 49.999999.

The entries of Table 3 show for a two-person game the probability of ruin and the expected duration of play for several values of p, q, X, and Y. The general outlines of the table are unmistakably clear.[9] Even when he has a 0.5 chance of winning, the gambler's chance of ruin is 0.9 when he has 10 percent of the total wealth, and rises to 0.99 when his share of the wealth falls to 1 percent. When the probability of the gambler's winning falls below 0.5, the probability of eventual ruin is practically certain, even when he initially possesses 10 percent of the wealth. The expected duration of play is highly sensitive to the probability that the gambler will win. When the gambler initially has 10 percent of the wealth, the expected duration of play before ruin is 900 trials. The expected duration falls to 50 when the probability of winning falls to 0.4 and falls to 30 when the probability of success falls to 0.33.

We can now examine the role that confiscatory rates of taxation play in the process of the accumulation and dissipation of wealth over time. An entrepreneur makes investments in alternatives whose

[9] Let p denote the probability that the gambler wins and q the possibility that he loses. If p = q, the probability that the gambler will become ruined is:

$$P_r = 1 - X/(X+Y). \text{ If } p \neq q,\ P_r = \frac{(q/p)^{(X+Y)} - (q/p)^X}{(q/p)^{(X+Y)} - 1}.$$

If p=q, the expected duration before ruin will be:

$$D_r = XY. \text{ If } p \neq q,\ D_r = \frac{X}{q-p} - \frac{X+Y}{q-p} \cdot \frac{1-(q/p)^X}{1-(q/p)^{(X+Y)}}.$$

future payoffs are uncertain. Sometimes he will win; sometimes he will lose (that is, the adversary will win); sometimes nobody will win (in other words, the entrepreneur will break even). Other things equal, the more progressive the rate of tax on winnings, the less willing an entrepreneur will be to take risks. The greater the rate of progressivity, the higher the excess tax on gains vis-à-vis losses. Under a proportional income tax, for instance, an income of $100,000 one year and zero the next will pay the same tax as annual incomes of $50,000 for two years. Under progressive taxation, however, the tax on $100,000 will be more than twice as large as the tax on $50,000.

Whereas an individual might be willing to make an investment with a probability of success on only, for example, 0.40 under proportional taxation, he might require a probability of success of, for example, 0.45 under progressive taxation. And the higher the rate of tax on winnings, the more favorable the odds must be before an entrepreneur will take the gamble. And the more favorable the odds to the gambler, the longer the expected duration of play before his ruin. If mobility within the distribution of income and wealth is considered more important than the shape of the distribution itself, high rates of tax become distinctly counterproductive in that they reduce the rate of personal mobility.

In the absence of inflation, government bonds would be a riskless investment. And if investments were truly riskless, the arithmetic of compound interest would exert itself. The higher the rate of tax on the accumulation of wealth, the more numerous will be the number of people who settle for lower, more certain returns. Fortunes are much less likely to erode under such circumstances. And the fortunes that do erode will erode at slower rates. On the one hand, high tax rates will encourage safe investments, which reduce the probability of ruin and lengthen the duration of time before ruin. On the other hand, by reducing the rate of mobility among wealth positions, high rates of tax also reduce the ability of newcomers to enter the high wealth brackets. On both grounds, then, high rates of tax encourage and promote the retention of large amounts of wealth in the hands of those who already have the wealth.[10]

High rates of taxation on incomes and estates produce results that are clearly inconsistent with expressed desires to make it

[10] It is noteworthy in the postwar period of confiscatory taxation that capital gains have been the primary route by which new private wealth has been amassed. Earnings taken in this form, of course, are subject to lower tax rates. Rather than being looked upon as a loophole, however, the capital gains provision should be looked upon as a second-best provision in our tax system, with considerably lower tax rates being first-best.

possible for all individuals to have reasonable opportunities to become wealthy. Present policies protect holders of previously accumulated wealth, both from themselves and from the competition of others who might otherwise amass new wealth. While such policies may penalize some holders of large wealth, they do not make any positive contribution to increasing the opportunity of all citizens to participate in the effort to accumulate wealth if they choose. The distinction between a tax system designed to penalize the wealthy and a tax system designed to assist the nonwealthy is critical, and is a theme to which we shall return in Chapter 5.

3
ECONOMIC EFFECTS OF TRANSFER TAXATION

It is often claimed that transfer taxation discourages saving and encourages contributing to philanthropic institutions. I shall examine these claims, and then consider how transfer taxation promotes fiscal illusion, thereby injecting an element of irrationality into our fiscal affairs.[1]

The Amount of Saving

It is often suggested that transfer taxation impinges on saving more strongly than other forms of taxation. We may view people who hold wealth upon entering the later years of their lives as choosing the amount of wealth they want to consume themselves and the amount they want to transfer to heirs. An increase in the rate of estate tax increases the price of providing for one's heirs relative to the price of providing for oneself. Since, following the first law of demand, the quantity of bequests purchased will fall as the price of bequests rises, an increase in estate tax rates should reduce the amount of wealth devoted to one's heirs relative to the amount devoted to oneself. Thus the estate tax would encourage dissaving by wealth holders, for dissaving is a means of avoiding estate tax. And transfer taxation, if it diminishes saving more strongly than other forms of taxation, will retard our rate of economic growth more severely than other forms of taxation.[2]

[1] The seminal work on fiscal illusion is Amilcare Puviani, *Die Illusionen in der öffentlichen Finanzwirtschaft*, trans. Marianne Hartmann and Felix Rexhausen (Berlin: Duncker & Humblot, 1960). For a brief English-language survey, see James M. Buchanan, *Public Finance in Democratic Process* (Chapel Hill: University of North Carolina Press, 1967), pp. 126-43.

[2] The effect of death taxation upon saving and economic growth is discussed in C. Lowell Harriss, "Revising Estate Taxation," *Tax Review*, vol. 32 (April 1971), pp. 15-16.

If rates of estate tax are set at 100 percent, the inducement to dissaving seems unambiguous. Under fully confiscatory taxation it is impossible to transfer wealth to heirs, so the individual is faced with a choice of leaving it to the state or consuming it himself.[3] Since the state is generally regarded with little affection, as attested by the paucity of bequests it receives, we should expect personal wealth to be consumed before death rather than be left for the state. We might expect that risk aversion combined with an inability to predict with certainty one's time of death would mean that some personal wealth would remain upon death. But we should also expect a greatly expanded use of annuities under such circumstances, which would virtually eliminate such remaining wealth.[4] When the rate of tax is 100 percent, there seems to be little question that estate taxation induces dissaving. And it seems but a simple extension of the argument to derive the same conclusion for intermediate cases: As the tax rate falls below 100 percent, saving would increase but would still be less than it would be in the absence of the estate tax.

We must be wary, however, of such facile use of interpolative reasoning. Saving for bequests has two dimensions, the amount transferred to successors and the amount transferred to government, and it is the sum of the two that is relevant for our analysis of saving. Although an increase in tax rate reduces the amount of wealth transferred to successors, it also increases the government's claim per unit of wealth. Suppose the estate tax rate is 50 percent, which means that a testator must pay a price of $1 for the right to transfer $1 to an heir. Thus the testator must save $2 of his wealth in order to transfer $1. Would a reduction in the tax rate to, say, 25 percent yield an increase, decrease, or no change in the amount of saving? The reduction in tax rate reduces the price of transferring wealth to heirs. With a 25 percent tax, a testator can transfer $1 to an heir by paying a price of only $0.32.

To the extent that saving is motivated by a demand for bequests, the impact of estate taxation upon saving will depend upon the testator's elasticity of demand for bequests. If the demand for bequests is inelastic, a reduction in tax rate (in other words, price of bequests) will reduce saving (that is, the amount spent purchasing bequests). Consider a reduction in tax rate from 50 percent to 25 percent, and assume that the elasticity of demand for bequests is zero. If $1 were transferred from a total saving of $2 with a 50 per-

[3] Unless transfers to nongovernmental institutions are exempt from tax.

[4] See, for instance, Gordon Tullock, "Inheritance Justified," *Journal of Law and Economics*, vol. 14 (October 1971), pp. 465-74.

cent tax rate, $1 will be transferred from a total saving of only $1.32 when the tax rate is reduced to 25 percent. If the demand for bequests is unit elastic, a change in tax rate will leave total saving unchanged. Hence, if $1 were transferred from a total saving of $2 with a tax rate of 50 percent, $1.50 will be transferred from a total saving of $2 when the tax rate is reduced to 25 percent. If the demand for bequests is elastic, a reduction in tax rate will increase total saving. If $1 were transferred from a total saving of $2 with a tax rate of 50 percent, something more than $2 will be saved and something more than $1.50 will be transferred when the tax rate is reduced to 25 percent, with the precise extent of increased saving dependent upon the actual elasticity of demand for bequests.

The preceding analysis suggests that the effect of the estate tax on saving is ambiguous. An increase in the rate of tax will increase saving by testators with inelastic demands for bequests, while the increase will reduce saving by testators with elastic demands. Despite this ambiguity, some general tendencies may be described. As a general proposition, the demand curve for any product becomes increasingly elastic as its price rises; even the most inelastic of demand curves must become elastic at some sufficiently high price. Where the marginal rate of tax is relatively low—on testators with relatively modest estates—the demand for bequests is likely to be relatively inelastic. Within this region, then, the estate tax is likely to increase the total amount of saving, though decreasing the amount of private saving. Where the marginal rate of tax is relatively high, by contrast, the demand for bequests is likely to be relatively elastic. In this case, which describes the situation faced by testators with relatively large amounts of wealth, the estate tax is likely to reduce the total amount of saving. While most testators face relatively low rates of tax, the highly skewed distribution of wealth suggests that the bulk of estates will be transferred by testators who face relatively high rates of tax. Hence, most wealth is likely to be transferred by testators who have relatively elastic demands for bequests, which indicates a strong likelihood that estate taxation reduces the amount of saving.

Contributions to Philanthropic Institutions

Analysis of the impact of estate taxation upon the volume of contributions to philanthropic institutions is similar to analysis of the impact of estate taxation upon saving. Given his decision about the amount of wealth to bequeath, we may view a testator as choosing to distribute his wealth between persons and institutions. In the

United States, gifts and bequests to a large number of charitable, educational, religious, and scientific institutions are exempt from tax.[5] Thus the estate tax is applicable to transfers made to persons but not to institutions. Because of this difference in tax treatment, it is commonly claimed that this exemption feature stimulates transfers to such eligible institutions as charities, churches, hospitals, and schools.[6] If this assertion is correct, the charitable deduction can be viewed as a way of subsidizing various nonprofit organizations.

However, it seems very likely that an increase in the rate of tax on estates will reduce bequests to charitable institutions by more than it will reduce bequests to persons. And since the preceding section of this chapter showed that an increase in the rate of estate tax will quite likely reduce total saving, the net result is that estate taxation will probably diminish contributions to philanthropic institutions. As with the case of saving, the analysis hinges upon relative elasticities of demand, in this case between bequests to persons and bequests to institutions.

It seems reasonable that most testators will place first priority on providing for their family rather than placing it on providing for institutions. Thus, generally, the family will be taken care of first, with others sharing the remainder of the estate with the government. The available evidence supports this presumption about testator behavior. The Treasury's special tabulations of estate tax returns for 1957 and 1959 show that charitable bequests were less than 4 percent of gross estates of less than $900,000, while noncharitable bequests were about 76 percent and taxes about 20 percent. Among estates exceeding $10 million, on the other hand, charitable bequests were about 30 percent, and noncharitable bequests and taxes about 35 percent each.[7]

As the average size of estates rise, bequests to institutions increase relative to bequests to persons. Such evidence as this suggests that testators look after their families first, with institutions receiving second consideration. Testators thus have relatively inelastic demands to transfer wealth to persons, and relatively elastic demands to transfer wealth to institutions. An increase in the rate of estate tax is an increase in the price of leaving wealth to individuals,

---

[5] Internal Revenue Code of 1954, Section 2055.

[6] See, for instance, Werner Z. Hirsch, *The Economics of State and Local Government* (New York: McGraw-Hill, 1970), p. 66; and Carl S. Shoup, *Public Finance* (Chicago: Aldine Publishing Co., 1969), p. 380.

[7] Robert Anthoine, "Testamentary Trusts," in Carl S. Shoup, *Federal Estate and Gift Taxes* (Washington: The Brookings Institution, 1966), p. 155.

so we should expect less wealth to be left. However, since the demand for bequests to persons is inelastic, the amount spent in making such transfers of wealth will increase. Since the total size of the estate is fixed, the residual amount of wealth left for charitable institutions will be reduced by an increase in tax rates.

The issue can be illustrated by a simple example. Assume a decedent during his lifetime decided to leave a target level of wealth to his family giving the remainder to charitable institutions. Suppose his target level of giving to persons is $300,000, and further suppose he would leave an estate of $1 million if the rate of tax were 33 percent. If the rate of tax is 33 percent, it will cost $150,000 to leave $300,000 for the family, and a residual of $550,000 will be left for charity. If the rate of tax is raised to 50 percent, the cost of leaving $300,000 for the family will rise to $300,000 which will reduce the residual left for charity to $400,000, assuming the total estate remains $1 million. To the extent that the increased tax rate reduces total saving, the residual transferred to philanthropic institutions will decline still further. An assumption of a target level of bequests to family members, of course, is an assumption of zero elasticity of demand, and was made only to simplify the arithmetical illustration. In the more general case of less than complete inelasticity, the rise in tax rate from 33 percent to 50 percent will reduce the amount transferred to the family to less than $300,000. Yet the amount of bequest plus the concomitant tax liability would still exceed $450,000, which would still leave less than $550,000 for charitable requests, again assuming that the increased tax rate did not reduce the total estate. If the increased tax rate reduces the total estate, the amount transferred as charitable bequests will decline even further. Therefore, the estate tax would seem to discourage, not encourage, bequests to charitable institutions.

Philanthropic institutions often compete directly with government in providing public-type goods. Private schools and universities compete with public institutions in educating the populace. Religious institutions and government compete in articulating cultural norms and common concerns, as well as in the undertaking of certain charitable activities. Private foundations compete with government agencies in sponsoring scientific research. By diminishing contributions to private philanthropic institutions, estate taxation promotes governmental monopoly over such areas. Yet concern for the maintenance of basic liberties, the preservation of minority preferences and points of view, and effectiveness in providing services all suggest that competition among institutions providing related services is preferable to monopoly.[8]

Rationality in Fiscal Choice

In a market economy firms compete among themselves for buyers, and it is generally acknowledged that the efficacy of market competition varies directly with the degree of awareness about alternatives possessed by the participants. Likewise, in a democracy politicians compete for voter support, and the efficacy of political competition will also vary directly with the awareness of the alternatives possessed by the citizenry. With respect to taxation, political competition will perform more effectively as voters perceive more accurately the tax costs of public services. There are several features about transfer taxation, however, that blur the clarity of taxpayer perceptions of cost.

It is widely acknowledged that inflation is a tax, as the reduction in the value of the dollar corresponds to the inflation-financed expenditures of the government.[9] But under progressive tax rates, inflation also increases the burden of income and transfer taxes by increasing the real rate of tax levied on income and wealth transfers. The federal estate tax initially became effective on 9 September 1916. At that time the range of coverage was small and the progression in tax rates was slight. After a $50,000 specific exemption, the rates ranged from one percent on the first $50,000 of taxable estate to 10 percent on the net taxable estate over $5 million. Table 4, which indicates briefly the historical development of the federal estate tax, documents the continual broadening and extension of the federal estate tax, particularly once we recognize that inflation has increased prices about 350 percent from their 1916 level.

Compared with 1916, for instance, the specific exemption has only been increased from $50,000 to $60,000. Yet merely to offset the erosion of purchasing power through inflation would now require a specific exemption of $175,000. The minimum rate of tax has increased from 1 to 3 percent, and the size of estate subject to the minimum rate has fallen from $50,000 in 1916 to $5,000 at present. Yet if we allow for inflation, the lowest rate bracket would now

---

[8] See William A. Niskanen, *Bureaucracy and Representative Government* (Chicago: Aldine Publishing Co., 1971), for discussion of many facets of these issues of competition and monopoly.

[9] Under fractional reserve banking, part of the tax is collected by the banking system rather than by the government.

Table 4
DEVELOPMENT OF FEDERAL ESTATE TAXATION

Internal Revenue Code of:	Specific Exemption ($ thousands)	Rate	Minimum On Taxable Estate Under: ($ thousands)	Rate	Maximum On Taxable Estate Over: ($ thousands)
1916	$ 50	1 %	$ 50	10%	$ 5,000
1917	50	1.5	50	15	5,000
1918	50	1	50	25	10,000
1924	50	1	50	25	10,000
1926	100	1	50	20	10,000
1932	50	1	10	45	10,000
1934	50	1	10	60	10,000
1935	40	2	10	70	50,000
1941	40	3	5	77	10,000
1942	60	3	5	77	10,000

Source: *Facts and Figures on Government Finance*, 15th ed. (New York: Tax Foundation, Inc., 1969), p. 112.

have to begin at $175,000 to maintain coverage comparable to that of 1916. Whereas the rate of tax on the lowest bracket has increased by 300 percent since 1916, it has increased by 770 percent in the highest rate bracket. Inflationary effects, however, have been partially offset, for the amount at which the maximum rate takes effect has been raised from $5 million to $10 million. A complete allowance for inflation, however, would require that the $10 million be increased to $17.5 million. As it stands now, estates that were valued at less than $3 million in 1916, and are still worth $3 million in terms of real purchasing power, would now be valued at $10 million due to nothing more than inflationary erosions in the value of money.[10]

In the absence of inflation, tax rates would have had to have been raised more sharply and coverage broadened more extensively to accomplish what was accomplished automatically through inflation. Yet it makes a difference whether taxes are increased through conscious modification of tax rates or through automatic adjustment resulting from inflation. Empirical evidence shows that people tend to take an unchanged rate and bracket structure rather than an

[10] The real tax rates of the gift tax have been increased in similar fashion by inflation, though the amounts are less because the present gift tax dates from the Revenue Act of 1932, and the price level has increased by only about 250 percent since then.

unchanged real rate of tax as evidence of an unchanged fiscal environment.[11] People are quite aware of conscious modification of tax rates, but are relatively unconscious of increases in tax rates that occur automatically through inflation. For evidence of this point, one need merely witness the strenuous discussion about the tax surcharge proposal of a few years ago, and compare that with the total failure to recognize that, *under progressive taxation, inflation imposes a similar surcharge each year.*[12]

Taxpayer perceptions about the real cost of public services also depend upon the structure of the tax system. Other things equal, cost in a tax system in which all revenues are raised by a single tax will be felt more strongly by taxpayers than one in which revenues are raised by numerous small taxes. Even though all taxpayers may bear the same tax burden whether they are subject to one larger tax or to ten smaller ones, they will tend to feel that public services are less costly when financed by the set of smaller taxes.[13] A tax provides a signal to the taxpayer at the moment of payment that he is losing income. People also forget, however, so perceptions about the tax become dulled with the passage of time between moments of payment. The clarity of the signal itself varies directly with its strength, so one larger tax will be forgotten less rapidly than ten smaller ones. Thus a taxpayer will tend to be more acutely aware of the real cost of public services when they are financed by one larger tax than by several smaller ones.

Estate and gift tax collections account for less than 3 percent of total federal tax collections. Such a relatively small tax can only contribute to fiscal illusion, thereby promoting some irrationality in the process of democratic fiscal choice. As a general principle of fiscal organization, fiscal choice will become more rational as the proliferation of tax bases is curtailed. This principle suggests that tax revenues ought to be collected from a single base, or at least ought not to rely upon numerous small bases. Estate and gift taxes violate this elementary principle of fiscal rationality.[14]

---

[11] Richard E. Wagner, *The Fiscal Organization of American Federalism* (Chicago: Markham Publishing Co., 1971), pp. 85-88.

[12] Three means exist for correcting the fiscal illusion created by inflation: restore price level stability, adopt proportional rates of tax, or define the bracket structure in real terms so that it is itself adjusted in response to changes in the price level.

[13] For a related discussion, though in a slightly different context, see Wagner, *Fiscal Organization*, pp. 52-54.

[14] For a more extensive examination of these issues concerning the proliferation of tax bases, see Richard E. Wagner, *The Public Economy* (Chicago: Markham Publishing Co., 1973), pp. 227-32.

4
TECHNICAL ISSUES CONCERNING TRANSFER TAXATION

In this chapter I shall consider five issues that are relatively more technical and more specific than those examined in Chapters 2 and 3: (1) whether transfer taxes should be of the estate or the inheritance form, (2) defining the unit upon which to base tax liability, (3) reducing tax avoidance through the creation of trusts, (4) difficulties associated with the liquidation of closely held businesses, and (5) strains created by the simultaneous taxation of transfers by forty-nine states and the federal government.

Taxation Upon Whom: Transferor or Transferee?

Assuming that a transfer of wealth from A to B and C gives rise to a tax liability, we can ask whether the tax should be levied upon A or upon B and C. This distinction defines the two contrasting forms of death taxation. If the tax is based upon the amount of wealth transferred by A, the transferor, we have the estate form of death taxation. If it is based upon the amount of wealth received by B and C, the transferees, we have the inheritance form of death taxation.

Taxation of the transferor—a unified transfer tax. In its 1969 proposals for tax reform, the Treasury recommended that the estate and gift taxes be combined into a unified tax on transfers. A single rate, bracket, and exemption schedule would apply to all transfers of wealth made by any transferor. The value of a donor's gifts would be cumulated over his lifetime as is done now, but the value of the estate would be added to the value of gifts to determine the total amount of taxable transfers.

Since gift tax rates are set at 75 percent of estate tax rates, it is commonly felt that transfers made by gifts receive more favorable treatment than transfers made by bequest. Supporters of a unified transfer tax contend that the lower rate of tax on gifts violates the principle of horizontal equity. Between two people who transfer the same amount of wealth to successors, the one who makes the more intensive use of gifts will pay less tax, and presumably thus be able to transfer a greater amount of wealth net of tax to his successors. Consider, as an illustration, two transferors, each with wealth of $1,244,275 to be transferred. If the wealth is transferred by bequest, the tax bill will be $420,967.25, which yields a net transfer of $823,306.75—ignoring for computational ease such complicating factors as exemptions. If the wealth is transferred by gift, by contrast, the tax bill will be only $244,275, which enables the donor to make a net transfer of $1,000,000. Thus among two people with equal wealth, the one who makes more extensive use of gifts will be able to transfer a greater amount of his wealth to successors.

It is doubtful, however, whether the lower tax rates on gifts should be considered a loophole, for relatively few donors find the lower rates a sufficient inducement to prefer gifts to bequests. Only those individuals with relatively strong preferences for maximizing the amount of wealth transferred to others will find a strong advantage in making gifts. In the absence of such preferences to maximize the amount of wealth transferred to successors, the prevailing rate differential between gifts and bequests does not seem significantly to subsidize inter vivos gifts.[1]

The case for an integrated transfer tax rests on two primary assumptions. First, that the amount of wealth transferred by the transferor is the appropriate base for taxation. This assumption is not widely held, except on a pragmatic basis. The preponderance of opinion seems to be that the amount of wealth received by the transferee is the more appropriate base for taxation. Yet while granting the conceptual superiority of taxation based upon the transferee, many acquiesce in taxation based on the transferor because it is administratively more convenient. Second, given the appropriateness of basing tax liability upon the size of the transferor's transfers, the assumption is made that better results are forthcoming under

[1] For careful analyses of these issues, see Harold M. Hochman and Cotton M. Lindsay, "Taxation, Interest, and the Timing of Inter-Generation Wealth Transfers," *National Tax Journal*, vol. 20 (June 1967), pp. 219-26; and Eli Schwartz and J. Richard Aronson, "The Preference for Accumulation vs. Spending: Gift and Estate Taxation and the Timing of Wealth Transfers," *National Tax Journal*, vol. 22 (September 1969), pp. 390-98.

a unified transfer tax. This assumption encapsulates the belief that a person who transfers $1 million during his life and $1 million upon his death should pay the same amount of tax as one who transfers $2 million upon his death, and that both should pay the same tax as one who transfers $2 million during his life. This argument might seem reasonable if interest rates were zero, but it seems unreasonable when interest rates are positive. Compare a transfer of $2 million during life with one of $2 million upon death ten years later. Since the tax payment is made ten years earlier in the case of the inter vivos gift than with the bequest, the tax payment on the gift exceeds the tax payment on the bequest because the interest that could have been earned had the tax not been paid was foregone over that ten-year period. If equal transfers of wealth are to be assigned the same present value of tax liability regardless of the timing of transfer, inter vivos gifts must be taxed at a lower rate than transfers upon death.

Taxation of the transferee—an accessions tax. Whereas liability for an estate tax depends on the size of the decedent's estate, liability for an inheritance tax depends on the amounts received by the heirs to the estate. An accessions tax is a unified tax on transfers, with liability based on the amounts received by transferees rather than the amounts given by transferors. An accessions tax, then, is a combination of inheritance tax plus gift tax on the donee. The base of an accessions tax would thus be an individual's total lifetime acquisitions through gifts and inheritances.

The primary rationale for accessions taxation is that the amount an individual receives is a better indicator of tax liability than the amount an individual gives. What matters is not the size of the decedent's estate, but the distribution of the estate among the heirs. With accessions taxation, an estate of $1 million that was left to a sole heir would pay a larger tax on its distribution than one that was distributed equally among ten heirs. Moreover, an estate of $10 million that was distributed equally among ten heirs would carry the same tax obligation as an estate of $1 million left to a single heir.

A subsidiary argument advanced in support of accessions taxation is that such a form of taxation will encourage a wider sharing of an estate because this is a means of reducing the tax levied upon the devolution of the estate. Large fortunes are thus less likely to be passed on from generation to generation under inheritance taxation than under estate taxation. This subsidiary argument, however, does not by itself support inheritance taxation because the same results can be attained under the estate form of taxation. All that would be necessary would be to establish a minimum exemption per bequest. If up to, say, $100,000 per legatee could be deducted from gross estate, inducement to wider sharing of estates would be given within the framework of estate taxation.

Although considerable feeling exists that it is preferable to base the tax on the amount received instead of on the amount transferred, inheritance taxation is subject to somewhat greater administrative cost than estate taxation. With an estate tax a single value is placed on the estate and the tax is determined. With an inheritance tax, however, a valuation must be placed on the share of each individual heir, and such valuation of individual shares is sometimes more difficult than valuation of the total estate. It is easier, for instance, to place a single value on all household effects than to first apportion the effects among separate heirs and then value each share. In most cases, of course, no significant differences in administrative cost will exist. But it can never be more costly to value an estate than to value separate inheritances, and there will occur occasions in which it is less costly to value the estate than the several inheritances.

Administrative issues aside, however, the primary argument given for an accessions tax over a unified transfer tax is that the size of an inheritance is a better index for basing tax obligations than the size of the estate from which the inheritance devolved.[2] As with the unified transfer tax, the case for an accessions tax rests on the assumption that the rate of interest is zero. Recognition that interest rates are positive creates a different perspective, and the impact on an accessions tax is the reverse of its impact on a unified transfer tax. With a unified transfer tax, equality of present values of tax liability requires a lower rate of tax on gifts than on bequests. With an accessions tax, by contrast, equality of present values of tax liability requires a higher rate of tax on gifts than on inheritances. Since the present value of a gift exceeds the present value of the same size inheritance received, for example, ten years later, the inheritance will be taxed more heavily than the gift if both transfers are subject to the same amount of tax. Therefore, equality of the present value of tax liability regardless of the timing of transfer requires that inheritances be taxed less heavily than gifts.

[2] Many people also feel that inheritance taxation is preferable because tax rates can be varied according to consanguinity. See, for instance, Dan T. Smith, *Federal Tax Reform* (New York: McGraw-Hill, 1961), p. 298. But an estate tax can achieve the same effect by allowing a per-legatee deduction that would vary according to consanguinity. Thus, for example, $200,000 could be deductible for transfers to sons and daughters, while only $100,000 could be deductible for transfers to nephews and nieces.

The Unit of Taxation

If a husband dies and is survived by his wife, should a tax be levied upon the husband's estate? The Internal Revenue Code of 1954 says "yes"; the Treasury's 1969 proposals for reform said "no." One's choice of the appropriate unit upon which to base tax liability depends primarily upon one's attitude toward the attribution of ownership. In some legal frameworks property is vested in the family unit rather than in the separate members of the family. Under such circumstances there can be no institution of inheritance, as the surviving members of the family unit cannot inherit what already belongs in common to the family unit.[3] Our legal framework recognizes and assigns individual ownership of property, so a decedent's property devolves upon someone else through succession—an institution that came into being only as societies came to recognize individual rather than family ownership of property.[4]

The federal estate tax recognizes individual rather than family ownership of property, though the 50 percent marital deduction represents a partial recognition of family ownership. Prior to the Revenue Act of 1942, deaths occurring in community property states were taxed less heavily than deaths occurring in common law states, for in community property states one-half of the husband's property acquired after marriage would be attributed to the wife, while in common law states all such property would be attributed to the husband. The Revenue Act of 1942 eliminated this differential treatment by treating deaths in community property states as if they occurred in common law states. The Revenue Act of 1948 maintained the equality of treatment, but did it by extending community property rights to deaths occurring in common law states by allowing a 50 percent marital deduction on noncommunity property.

Even with the 50 percent marital deduction, two families of identical wealth can bear different tax liabilities, depending upon

---

[3] See, for instance, Shultz's description of the Hindu joint-family system in which there is no inheritance because property is owned in common by the family and is acquired by survivorship rather than by succession. William J. Shultz, *The Taxation of Inheritance* (Boston: Houghton-Mifflin, 1926), p. 33.

[4] Eugene F. Scoles and Edward C. Halbach, Jr., *Problems and Materials on Decedent's Estates and Trusts* (Boston: Little, Brown & Co., 1965), p. 5. Moreover, the particular rules of inheritance used by a society will reflect its attitudes toward the nature of the family and its individual members. A patriarchal society will emphasize succession through the male line, for instance, whereas a matriarchal society will emphasize succession through the female line. See George W. Paton, *A Textbook of Jurisprudence*, 3rd ed. (Oxford: Oxford University Press, 1964), p. 493.

whether the richer or poorer spouse dies first. Take the case of a noncommunity property state in which the husband's wealth is $1,000,000 and the wife's is zero. If the husband predeceases the wife, the marital deduction can be taken by the wife, which would reduce the husband's gross estate to $500,000. If the wife dies first, however, no marital deduction can be taken, so the gross estate upon the husband's death would be $1,000,000. Thus the base splitting permitted by the marital deduction can be exploited only if the wealthier spouse dies first. The order of death can make a substantial difference in tax liability: The tax on a taxable estate of $1,000,000 is $325,700, while the total tax on two taxable estates of $500,000 each is $291,400.

The Treasury's 1969 proposals for transfer tax reform, by suggesting that the 50 percent limit on the marital deduction be removed, went a considerable distance toward recognizing the family as the unit of taxation. Ownership would still be attributed to individual members of the family, and a tax liability would potentially be created upon the death of any member of the family. But the family would have available the option of making tax-free transfers between husband and wife.[5]

Full marital exemption now commands wide support, for it is unreasonable to treat the surviving members of a family as receiving a capital gain when one member dies. Since the family is usually considered the basic unit of ownership de facto, even though not de jure, the surviving members of the family do not acquire additional nonhuman capital by virtue of one member's death. Furthermore, the family has suffered a reduction in the stock of human capital available to it. The death of the father sharply reduces the income available to support the family; the death of the mother sharply

[5] U.S. Treasury Department, *Tax Reform Studies and Proposals*, vol. 5 (Washington: U.S. Government Printing Office, February 1969), pp. 357-60. Circumstances are conceivable under which tax liability will be greater with a 100 percent marital deduction than with a 50 percent deduction. Consider the case of a husband who dies and leaves $1,000,000 to his wife, who in turn dies within two years. Further assume the wife consumed only the income from her inheritance. Under 100 percent marital deduction, no tax is levied upon the husband's death, while $325,700 is levied upon the wife's death, assuming for arithmetic convenience that the entire estate was taxable. Under 50 percent marital deduction, by contrast, a tax of $145,700 is levied upon the husband's $500,000 and a tax of $271,791 is levied upon the wife's $854,300. Since the wife died within two years of the husband, however, her estate will be credited with 100 percent of her husband's estate tax payment under the provision for quick succession relief. Thus the net tax on the wife's estate is $126,091, producing a total tax of $271,791 on the devolution of the estate, which is $53,909 less tax than with 100 percent marital deduction.

increases the cost of maintaining the family because many of the services provided free by the mother must now be purchased. By treating the family (husband, wife, and dependent children) as the unit of taxation, a tax would be levied as property devolved from the family unit. No tax liability would result from the death of one member of the family so long as there was a surviving member.[6] Such a change would bring the unit upon which tax liability is based into consistency with prevailing attitudes about the appropriate unit of ownership of property. A transfer tax should be levied, if one is to be levied at all, only if there is a clear capital gain to the recipient—and this requires adoption of the family as the unit of taxation.

Generation-Skipping Trusts[7]

The amount of tax levied upon the devolution of an estate will depend upon the form by which the estate is transferred. Consider two different ways of transferring the same estate from father to son to grandson. In the first case let the father transfer $1 million to his son, who lives on the interest income and transfers the remainder to the grandson. The father's estate pays a tax of $325,700 (assuming again for convenience that all figures are taxable amounts), leaving $674,300 to the son. The son lives off the interest from the estate, and transfers the principal amount to the grandson. A tax of $206,705 is levied upon the son's estate, which leaves $467,595 for the grandson. Thus the total tax bill on the devolution of the estate from the father to the grandson via the son is $532,405.

In the second case let the father transfer the $1 million in trust to the grandson, giving the son a life tenancy in the income from the estate. The father's estate again pays a tax of $325,700, which leaves $674,300 in trust for the grandson. Again the son lives off the income from $674,300, but since he does not have title to the property, no tax is levied upon his death. The grandson now receives $674,300, so the generation-skipping trust has reduced the tax liability on the devolution of the estate by $206,705. Yet the two cases are identical in all essential respects.

---

[6] For an early treatment of succession defined in terms of the family unit, see Harold M. Groves and Wallace I. Edwards, "A New Model for an Integrated Transfer Tax," *National Tax Journal*, vol 4 (December 1953), pp. 353-60. For a more recent statement, see Joseph A. Pechman, *Federal Tax Policy* (Washington: The Brookings Institution, 1966), 183-87.

[7] For an extensive survey of trusts and their relation to estate taxation, see Gerald R. Jantscher, *Trusts and Estate Taxation* (Washington: The Brookings Institution, 1967).

Generation-skipping trusts are a modern, though limited, version of primogeniture. Under primogeniture, the eldest son received a life tenancy in the estate, which in turn was passed on to his son, and this pattern of succession continued until either the nation or the family died out. For the most part, generation-skipping trusts are limited only by the rule against perpetuities, which says that interest designated in the trust must vest not later than 21 years after the death of the last person alive at the time of the creation of the trust.[8]

By making the tax liability depend merely on the form of transfer, trusts generate horizontal inequity. By creating a life tenancy rather than bequeathing the corpus, trusts retard the dissipation of large holdings of wealth, reduce risk-taking, and retard the rate of capital mobility. On all these grounds, generation-skipping trusts have undesirable consequences. Yet trusts do serve important functions, so the task is to tax trusts more effectively, not to preclude their use, although more effective taxation will certainly curtail their use. To maintain a sense of perspective, however, we should note that the magnitudes involved are relatively small. Using Internal Revenue Service special tabulations for millionaire decedents, Robert Anthoine found that about 11 percent of gross transfers skipped one generation and about 3 percent skipped more than one generation.[9] Although trusts clearly raise issues about horizontal equity and allocative efficiency, it is also important to recognize that generation-skipping trusts represent a relative trickle in the overall devolution of estates, rather than a flood.

The salient way of taxing trusts is to levy an estate tax upon the death of the life tenant, with the remainder distributed to the remaindermen. Consider as an example a father who leaves a post-tax estate of $1 million in trust to his four grandchildren, with his two sons as life tenants. The sons share the trust income equally, and upon the death of the last surviving son the estate passes out of trust to be divided equally among the grandsons. If the sons should die simultaneously, an estate tax would be levied upon the $1 million corpus, with the remainder distributed equally among the grandsons. Or if one son dies before the other, an estate tax would be levied upon $500,000 of the corpus. Upon the death of the surviving son, a tax would be levied upon the remaining corpus.

Two major objections have been brought against proposals to tax the corpus upon the death of the life tenant. One is largely

---

8 Foundations, which are also a form of primogeniture, are not covered by the rule against perpetuities.

9 Robert Anthoine, "Testamentary Trusts," pp. 162-63.

imaginary and one is quite real. On the imaginary level, many claim that it is unfair to levy a full estate tax upon the expiry of the life tenant because the life tenant has not had control over the corpus of the trust.[10] Actually, the life tenant often has considerable opportunity to invade the corpus. Moreover, a policy of levying an estate tax upon the death of the life tenant will itself produce subsequent changes in the pattern of bequests, and judgments of equity must be based on this probable alternative pattern rather than on the prevailing pattern. Taxing the corpus upon the death of the life tenant reduces the relative advantage of leaving estates in trust. Since the advantage of using trusts would be lessened, more bequests would be made outright. Thus taxation upon death of the life tenant would itself reduce the magnitude of the problem by reducing the use of trusts as an instrument for making bequests.

A quite real difficulty in taxing the expiration of life estates lies in the creation of discretionary trusts. Under a discretionary trust, the shares of the various life tenants are not specified in advance, but are left to the discretion of the trustee, although he and the decedent may have in fact agreed upon a specific sharing scheme. If four life tenants share the income from a $1 million discretionary trust, the death of one tenant does not produce an unambiguous increase in the share available to the others. Since the tenants are not assigned individual shares in the estate, it is impossible to specify the increase in the share available to the remaining tenants that results from the death of one tenant. By contrast, if the trust were equally shared among the life tenants, the death of one tenant would increase by $250,000 the amount available to the others. Perhaps the most appealing way of overcoming this problem is to use Gerald Jantscher's look-back approach, under which, roughly, a share of the trust is imputed to a life tenant in the same proportion that the tenant's income from the trust, over some specified period, was to the total income from the trust, over that same period.[11]

---

[10] See, for instance, Pechman, *Federal Tax Policy*, pp. 191-95.

[11] Jantscher, *Trusts and Estate Taxation*, pp. 172-90. There are other ways available for taxing generation-skipping trusts. The Treasury's proposals for reform suggested that a substitute tax be placed on the corpus of generation-skipping trusts, with the tax rate set at some fraction of the testator's estate tax rate. It would also be possible to tax trusts by treating the trustee as the owner of the corpus. Thus when the final life tenant died and the estate passed out of trust, the corpus would be treated as if it passed from one owner (the trustee) to another (the remaindermen). There are many alternative forms for trust taxation, none of which will be perfect, but some of which might be preferable to prevailing institutions.

Liquidity Problems of Closely Held Businesses

The liquidation of assets to pay estate tax sometimes creates special difficulties when the assets are not readily marketable, which is often true with closely held businesses. Considerable evidence suggests that the need to liquidate the assets of closely held businesses to pay estate tax encourages mergers of such businesses with larger corporations. Chelcie Bosland, for instance, estimated that in 63 percent of mergers of closely owned businesses over the period 1955-1959, estate tax considerations played a significant factor in the decision to merge.[12] Two separate motivations seem to lie behind the desire to merge closely owned businesses. On the one hand, there is a fear that the estate will have insufficient liquidity to pay the tax, and merger is a source of liquidity. On the other hand, the amount of tax liability to be assessed is itself uncertain because it depends upon an arbitrary valuation of the business by the Internal Revenue Service, so this uncertainty also creates a demand for liquidity.[13]

Estate tax law permits the executor of an estate to request that liquidation be allowed to take place over a period of up to ten years. This provision would seem to mitigate the problems of liquidation and the mergers produced thereby. The provision for deferred liquidation has had little impact, however, because it is not available unless the executor assumes personal responsibility for all future tax payments, regardless of what should happen to the value of the estate's assets in the interim. Thus the need to liquidate closely owned businesses in order to pay estate tax remains a serious problem. By suggesting that the personal liability for deferred taxes be removed from the executor by giving the government a security interest in the assets for which deferred payment is sought, the Treasury's 1969 proposals for reform took a significant step toward alleviating this problem.[14]

12 Chelcie C. Bosland, "Has Estate Taxation Induced Recent Mergers?" *National Tax Journal*, vol. 16 (June 1963), pp. 159-68. For earlier assessments that reach the same conclusions, see Harold M. Somers, "Estate Taxes and Business Mergers," *Journal of Finance*, vol. 13 (May 1958), pp. 201-10; and Wilbur A. Steger, "The Taxation of Unrealized Capital Gains and Losses: A Statistical Study," *National Tax Journal*, vol. 10 (September 1957), pp. 266-81.

13 Tax liability also depends upon random fluctuations in stock prices. Since stock prices are sometimes subject to considerable fluctuation over short periods of time, estates composed of identical holdings of stock may carry significantly different valuations because of a few days difference in the time of death. See C. Lowell Harriss, "Stock Prices, Death Tax Revenues, and Tax Equity," *Journal of Finance*, vol. 5 (September 1950), pp. 257-69.

14 U.S. Treasury, *Tax Reform Studies and Proposals*, pp. 401-08.

Closely related to this liquidity problem is the avoidance of capital gains tax on assets that are held until death. While unrealized capital gains are taxed as part of the decedent's estate, they escape liability for income tax and the successor is allowed to revalue the assets at their present market value. In its 1969 proposals for reform, the Treasury recommended that appreciated capital gains on assets transferred upon death be subject to ordinary capital gains taxation.[15] The application of capital gains taxation to assets transferred upon death may counteract some of the "lock-in" effect of unrealized capital gains, thereby increasing the rate of capital mobility in the economy. A policy of taxing unrealized capital gains upon death, however, will aggravate the liquidity problems of closely held businesses, as the tax liability would be increased significantly in relation to the available liquidity.[16] The choice among alternative approaches to capital gains taxation is especially difficult to resolve because all of the alternatives represent the horns of a dilemma. In his careful examination of the available alternatives, Harold Somers concluded that two primary alternatives exist: (1) tax capital gains upon death, or (2) exempt capital gains during life.[17] That neither can be considered ideal attests to the depth of the dilemma.

Federal-State Concurrent Taxation

In addition to the federal estate and gift taxes, forty-nine states levy inheritance or estate taxes and twelve levy gift taxes. Considerable complexity is sometimes created in tax compliance as a result. A person who maintains a part-time residence in a second state may be claimed as a resident by both states for death tax purposes. Or shares of corporation stock may be taxed both by the state in which the decedent was domiciled and the state in which the corporation is chartered. Such possibilities for overlapping taxation place a cost

---

[15] Ibid., pp. 28-29. For an estimation that full taxation of unrealized capital gains would have increased tax revenues in 1967 by $1.9 billion, see Peter Eilbott, "The Revenue Gain From Taxation of Decedent's Unrealized Capital Gains," *National Tax Journal*, vol. 22 (December 1969), pp. 506-15.

[16] On the average, about one-half of unrealized capital gains are held in either real estate or shares of ownership in unincorporated enterprises. Moreover, the relative holdings of these asset classes fall as wealth rises. A policy of taxing unrealized capital gains upon death would thus impinge more forcefully upon the liquidity position of estates in the middle wealth ranges than in the higher wealth ranges.

[17] Harold M. Somers, "Taxation of Capital Gains at Death," in Paul L. Kleinsorge, ed., *Public Finance and Welfare* (Eugene: University of Oregon Press, 1966), pp. 135-55.

on individuals by inducing them to conduct their affairs so as to avoid such double taxation.

Many people feel that the diversity in state death tax laws introduces excessive complexity into tax compliance. This has led to the suggestion that greater uniformity among the states is a desirable objective of federal policy on death taxation. The simplest way of attaining this objective is to have federal preemption of death taxation.[18] Instead of federal preemption, some people suggest that the federal credit for state death tax payments be used more strenuously to promote greater uniformity among states.[19]

The federal credit for state death taxes initially appeared with the Revenue Act of 1924, and was set at a rate of 25 percent. The rate of credit was increased to 80 percent with the enactment of the Revenue Act of 1926. With the passage of the Revenue Act of 1932, which increased federal estate tax rates considerably, the rate of credit was maintained at 80 percent, but only 80 percent of what would have been estate tax liability under the Revenue Act of 1926. This peculiar subterfuge continued until the Revenue Act of 1954 brought the credit into conformity with prevailing practice; the amounts of credit were not changed, but the computation was based upon prevailing death tax schedules rather than upon what would have taken place under 1926 schedules.

The federal credit for state death tax payments could be modified to encourage greater uniformity in state death taxation. To this end the Advisory Commission on Intergovernmental Relations (ACIR) recommended a three-part reform of the federal credit.[20] First, it recommended a two bracket credit: A credit of 80 percent would be allowed on the first $250,000 of taxable estate and 20 percent on the remainder. Second, the ACIR recommended that the credit be given only for the estate-type of death tax. Third, it recommended that the states be required to practice revenue maintenance for the following five years by certifying that its own death tax collections were not reduced to offset the additional credit.

The credit device could be used even more strenuously to encourage uniformity than the proposal to give credit only for

---

[18] See, for example, Shoup, *Federal Estate and Gift Taxes*, pp. 84-85.

[19] See the report of the Advisory Commission on Intergovernmental Relations, *Coordination of State and Federal Inheritance, Estate, and Gift Taxes* (Washington: U.S. Government Printing Office, 1961); and James A. Maxwell's discussion of it, "A New Proposal for Coordination of Death Taxation," *National Tax Journal*, vol. 14 (December 1961), pp. 382-87.

[20] Advisory Commission on Intergovernmental Relations, *Coordination of State and Federal Inheritance, Estate, and Gift Taxes*, pp. 16-21.

estate-type taxes. More detailed specification of the format of the estate tax would be possible. The base of the state's tax that would be eligible for credit could be specified. The most complete instance of federally imposed uniformity would result from a tax supplement, under which a state simply makes its death tax collections some percentage of the decedent's federal tax liability by a supplement of the federal estate tax. In this way the federal government would exercise considerable control over the form of state death taxation, and such control might serve as the first step toward federal preemption of death taxation.[21]

Support for federal preemption of the death tax field is based upon a desire to eradicate instances of overlapping taxation by two or more states. Some who take this position suggest the federal government share with the states the revenues they preempt, while others do not. In either event this consideration is an incidental matter, for the case for federal preemption seems flimsy. In the first place, double taxation is the exception, not the rule. So federal preemption is a steep price to pay for avoiding a few cases of double taxation. Most cases of double taxation can be handled adequately through the legal system. At one time the Supreme Court had specified a relatively simple set of standards to govern state death taxation: realty and tangible property would be taxed in the state of location and intangible property would be taxed in the state of domicile.[22] By refusing to assign single domiciliary for tax purposes, the Court has since backed away from this principle, thereby contributing to the increased complexity of state death taxation over the past thirty years. At the same time, however, it seems clear that legal modifications can contribute to simplicity in state death taxation. And, moreover, even should the law permit double taxation, it is not clear that serious problems are created so long as prospective decedents are aware of the law. For instance, since the problems that may arise with multiple domiciliary are well known, prospective decedents have the opportunity to arrange their affairs to avoid double taxation.

People in general seem to have a strong fixation with hierarchical orderings. With respect to taxation, it quite naturally seems neater

---

[21] Maxwell, "Proposal for Coordination of Death Taxation," suggested that it would be desirable to use the federal credit to promote greater uniformity among the states as a first step toward attaining the ultimate goal of complete federal jurisdiction over transfer taxation.

[22] William J. Shultz and C. Lowell Harriss, *American Public Finance*, 8th ed. (Englewood Cliffs, N.J.: Prentice-Hall, 1965), pp. 377-78.

to have one set of tax provisions than fifty-one. But this is a line of argument that is true for anything, whether it be tax laws, brands of cereal, styles of clothing, or news stories. However, uniformity in tax institutions, as uniformity elsewhere, is purchased at a price. And the price of federal preemption seems quite steep, especially since the alleged benefits are small and the problems can be handled in other ways.[23]

[23] For a good description of credits, supplements, and intergovernmental agreements as alternative ways of securing greater uniformity in state death taxation, see William H. Sager, "Practicability of Uniform Death and Gift Tax Laws," *National Tax Journal*, vol. 10 (December 1957), pp. 361-69.

5
A FRAMEWORK FOR FISCAL REFORM

In this chapter I want to examine some fundamental, long-run issues concerning reform in the taxation of wealth transfers. I shall do this by comparing the incorporation of transfers into the personal income tax with the maintenance of separate provisions for taxing transfers of wealth.

Incorporating Transfers into the Personal Income Tax

Section 102 of the Internal Revenue Code of 1954 specifically excludes from the definition of income any wealth received by gift or inheritance. However, personal income is commonly defined as the maximum amount of real consumption over some period of time that could be undertaken without reducing the real value of capital. In other words, personal income is equal to consumption during the year plus wealth at the end of the year minus wealth at the beginning of the year.[1] Consistent application of this definition of income suggests that inheritances or gifts are income to the recipient. If a person with an annual income of $20,000 and a beginning wealth of $100,000 has an ending wealth of $600,000 due to the inheritance of $500,000, his income for the year would be $520,000.[2] Elementary principles of consistency would seem to make a strong case for

[1] See Henry C. Simons, *Personal Income Taxation* (Chicago: University of Chicago Press, 1938), p. 50.

[2] That is, $520,000 = $20,000 + $600,000 — $100,000.

abandoning separate taxes on wealth transfers and treating inheritances and gifts as income under the personal income tax.[3]

If gifts are considered income to the donee and if inheritances are considered income to the legatee, the question arises as to whether such transfers should be considered as a loss of income to the transferor. While the usual presumption is that such transfers should not be deductible from the income of the transferor, there are strong reasons for suggesting that such transfers should be deductible. Consider a donee whose beginning wealth was $50,000, whose consumption during the year was $15,000, and whose ending wealth was $100,000, with the increased wealth reflecting a gift of $50,000. His income for the year is clearly $65,000. Further suppose the donor's beginning wealth was $200,000, his consumption during the year was $40,000, and his ending wealth was $150,000, with the reduced wealth reflecting his gift of $50,000. Using Henry Simons' definition of income, the donor's income is −$10,000. Consistent application of this definition of income suggests that while gifts should be counted as income to the donee, they ought to be counted as losses of income to the donor.[4] As a matter of administrative convenience, however, it would probably be simpler to ignore gifts completely unless they occur within some minimal period of time before the donor's death, in which case gifts would be treated as inheritances.

The principles regarding gifts from the standpoint of the donor and the donee are also applicable to bequests from the standpoint of the legator and the legatee. Consider a legator whose initial wealth was $200,000, whose consumption before his death was $20,000, and whose wealth at the end of the year was zero—reflecting the devolution of his estate to legatees. A consistent application of the definition of income would suggest that the legator's income for that year was −$180,000. Since negative incomes are not recognized by the personal income tax, his income for the year for tax purposes

[3] The classic presentation of this position was developed by Simons. See Simons, *Personal Income Taxation*, pp. 125-47. The Income Tax Act of 1894, by the way, proposed to incorporate gifts and inheritances into the definition of personal income.

[4] This was not Simons' position, however, for he did not want to permit transferors to reduce their income by transferring wealth. For his reasoning, see Ibid., pp. 56-58 and 134-40. The provisions of the personal income tax that allow deductions for transfers to philanthropic institutions are compatible with this line of reasoning, though the current practice of allowing deduction for transfers to institutions but not to persons is perhaps an unfortunate practice in an increasingly impersonal society.

should be zero, whereas it would be $20,000 under prevailing practices.

A logical and consistent application of the generally preferred definition of income suggests that gifts and inheritances should be treated as income to the transferees and treated as losses of income to the transferors. Separate provisions for the taxation of wealth transfers are incompatible with a consistent application of the definition of income. Moreover, the treatment of transfers as income and the elimination of special provisions for transfer taxation is more in accord with the functions of a tax system which were examined in Chapter 1. This is so both for financing the supply of public services and for transferring income. Considerations of horizontal equity in the assignment of tax liability to finance the supply of general-benefit public services reinforce the view that separate transfer taxation is unwarranted. Taxation based on either the size of an estate or the size of an inheritance will often result in people with equal incomes paying unequal taxes, due merely to differences among persons in the source of their income.

However, if gifts and inheritances are to be treated as income to the recipient, it becomes exceedingly important to develop expanded provisions for averaging income, at least so long as income is taxed at progressive rates. If income were taxed at proportional rates, there would be no reason for averaging because persons with fluctuating incomes would pay the same tax as persons with constant incomes. But with progressive taxation in the absence of averaging, a person with a fluctuating income would pay a greater tax than a person with a constant income, even though the present values of both income streams were identical. In the absence of averaging, a married person filing a joint return who had a taxable income of $10,000 for four years and $60,000 for one year—the additional $50,000 representing an inheritance—would pay a total tax of $29,580 on the total taxable income of $100,000. By contrast, a married person filing a joint return who had a taxable income of $20,000 per year for five years would pay a total tax of $21,900 on his $100,000 of taxable income. Hence, ignoring for computational simplicity possible differences in present values as between the two persons, the person with the fluctuating income would pay $7,680 more tax on the same income over the five-year period than the person with the constant income. Moderate averaging has been part of the personal income tax since the Revenue Act of 1964. However, if gifts and inheritances should be treated as income under the personal income tax, substantial fluctuations in personal income would become much more prevalent due to the irregular receipts of gifts and inheritances. Therefore, equity in taxation would require that the period for averaging income be extended beyond five years.

Maintaining Separate Provisions for Transfer Taxation

While some support probably exists for treating gifts and inheritances as income, Joseph A. Pechman is probably correct in stating that "tax theorists almost unanimously agree that estate and gift taxation should play a larger role in the revenue system." [5] For instance, during the 1965 Brookings conference on estate and gift taxation, little support was found for incorporating gifts and inheritances into the personal income tax.[6] Yet gifts and inheritances are income. Since income is widely regarded as the most appropriate source of general revenue, it is difficult to comprehend the strong endorsement given to estate and gift taxation as separate institutions.

The maintenance of separate provisions for the taxation of wealth transfers must be supported by some argument to the effect that the source of a person's wealth is a legitimate object upon which to base differences in tax treatment among individuals. It is sometimes suggested that "earned" wealth is more legitimate than inherited wealth,[7] though it is never said just how being born with great athletic ability, a glib tongue, a pleasing singing voice, good looks, high intellect, or a charismatic presence on television can be said to be "earned." Such a suggestion concerning the inferiority of inherited wealth leads to proposals for special taxation of wealth transfers. Using the jargon of modern welfare economics, if some people are envious of those who inherit wealth while no one is envious of those who "earn" their wealth, Pareto-optimality requires that this envy be assuaged via inheritance taxation.[8]

While the sanctification of envy via taxation may be argued by using the vocabulary of welfare economics, such tautological usage

---

[5] Pechman, *Federal Tax Policy*, p. 200.

[6] Shoup, *Federal Estate and Gift Taxes*, p. 200. Nonetheless, the 1966 report of the Carter Commission on comprehensive tax reform in Canada recommended that gifts and inheritances be taxed as income to the recipients. See "Taxation of Income," *Report of the Royal Commission on Taxation*, vol. 3 (Ottawa: Queen's Printer, 1966), pp. 465-519.

[7] See, for example, Lester C. Thurow, *The Impact of Taxes on the American Economy* (New York: Praeger Publishers, Inc., 1971), pp. 157-58.

[8] Such an argument for using taxation to assuage envy appears in E. J. Mishan, "A Survey of Welfare Economics," *The Economic Journal*, vol. 70 (June 1960), pp. 197-256.

illustrates only the sterility of modern welfare economics. To discuss inheritance with such an analytical framework is to evade most of the issues worth discussing, for the "conclusions" reached by such analysis are implied by the initial premises. Moreover, the acceptance of such modes of analysis precludes any analysis of the properties of a social order operating under different institutions with respect to inheritance. It is far more productive to focus an analysis of inheritance on the comparative properties of social orders operating with and without inheritance. When John Stuart Mill observed that the maintenance of a free society requires "liberty of tastes and pursuits . . . without impediment from our fellow-creatures, so long as what we do does not harm them, even though they should *think* our conduct foolish, perverse, or wrong,"[9] he implicitly established a much richer agenda concerning the institution of inheritance than can ever be established by using the analytical modes of welfare economics. As Mill saw it, the legitimization of envy was inconsistent with the maintenance of a free society; merely to be emotionally affronted by someone cannot be legitimate grounds for legislation if a free society is to survive. While Mills' prognosis may be incorrect on this point, and while there are numerous questions concerning the concrete implication of his dictum, the important point is that an altogether different agenda is established for examining such social institutions as inheritance, an agenda against which the impoverishment of modern welfare economics is starkly exposed.

The issue concerning the social function of inheritance revolves around an analysis of two alternative social orders, one operating with inheritance and one operating without. If inheritance were abolished, some envy would perhaps be assuaged. But there are also several positive features of a social order in which inheritance is sanctioned that would be destroyed if inheritance were abolished.

The abolition of inheritance would reduce saving, and hence capital formation and economic progress, as was described in Chapter 3. As a consequence of this impact, some subtle changes would take place in our society, changes that would occur slowly but with considerable force in the long run. Without inheritance, characteristics compatible with the accumulation of wealth would have less survival value in our society relative to such characteristics as pleasing superiors, scoring well on examinations, and appearing personable in public. Hence over time we should expect to find a reduction in those characteristics that are compatible with accumulating wealth.

[9] "On Liberty," in his *Utilitarianism, Liberty, and Representative Government*, Everyman's Library, No. 482 (London: Dent, 1910 [1859]), p. 75 (my italics).

Yet in a free enterprise economy, those who become relatively wealthy are to a considerable extent those who have been relatively more successful in producing services valued highly by other people; the more a person is able to provide services to others that are highly valued by the recipients, the wealthier the provider will become. The characteristic of providing valuable services to others has higher survival value in a social order that permits inheritance than in one that does not, and it would seem quite important to promote the survival of this characteristic rather than to promote its extinction.[10]

Furthermore, the institution of inheritance makes possible the establishment of private sources of wealth. Therefore, inheritance makes it possible for private wealth to compete with public wealth in undertaking a variety of artistic, cultural, educational, philanthropic, and scientific activities. Without competition from private wealth, government would exercise a monopoly over such areas of life. Yet the maintenance of diversity so that minority views may survive and possess a chance of becoming majority views seems a necessary ingredient of a free society. Inheritance promotes such diversity by preventing monopoly control over the financing of such spheres of life.

Moreover, transfers of wealth reflect an interdependence of utility functions between transferor and transferee.[11] That a legator could have purchased an annuity and left no estate, but chose to leave the estate instead, reflects the existence of an affective bond among generations. Gifts reflect such affective bonds perhaps even more strongly. What is the impact of taxing an essentially benevolent activity? One might indeed wish to tax activities that reflect hate, but why activities that reflect love? Currently, little is understood as to how social institutions, by generating selective information through experience, induce changes in preferences. Yet social institutions clearly have such an impact. It seems not at all unreasonable to suspect that one impact of the abolition of inheritance would be to diminish intergenerational bonds, with potentially far-reaching consequences for the character of the social order.

Leaving aside possible changes in preferences, the abolition of inheritance will generate a demand for substitute institutions, thereby creating some excess burden from the resulting adaptations. Inheri-

---

[10] For a seminal examination of the way in which an institutional framework promotes the survival of certain characteristics and not of others, see Armen A. Alchian, "Uncertainty, Evolution, and Economic Theory," *Journal of Political Economy*, vol. 58 (June 1950), pp. 211-21.

[11] For a careful exposition of utility interdependence, see Harold M. Hochman and James D. Rodgers, "Pareto Optimal Redistribution," *American Economic Review*, vol. 59 (September 1969), pp. 542-57.

tance results because transferors have a demand for making transfers of wealth. The prohibition of inheritance does not diminish this demand, but rather establishes a disequilibrium situation in much the same manner as, for example, rent ceilings. If the inheritance of wealth were precluded, adaptations would take place to generate other forms of inheritance in much the same manner as selling furniture to tenants and reduced maintenance of premises is an adaptation to rent ceilings. One possible adaptation to the abolition of inheritance would be an increased inheritance of occupational positions, much as is now practiced by a few labor unions. If such inherited positions were combined with an expanded use of employment tenure, social mobility would be retarded and the social order would come to be based relatively more on caste or status.[12]

There seems little doubt that much support for separate provisions for transfer taxation is due to a genuine concern for assisting those who have been left out of the mainstream of the American economy. Yet there is a fundamental difference between a tax policy designed to penalize the relatively fortunate and a tax policy designed to assist the relatively unfortunate. While high marginal rates of tax may penalize the wealthy, they do not significantly assist the nonwealthy to become wealthier.

Attempts to penalize the fortunate via high marginal rates of tax distort the allocation of resources in several directions, creating a substantial excess burden. High marginal rates of tax reduce the willingness of investors to undertake risky investments, which decreases the rate of mobility of individuals within the distribution of income. Consequently, the wealthy are more likely to stay wealthy and the poor are less likely to become wealthy. Moreover, nominally high rates of estate taxation promote a considerable investment in estate planning to avoid tax. Not only are revenues collected by government, but also considerable investment is made in estate planning, and the investment in the latter is the deadweight loss associated with collecting the former. Taxes are collected on monetary transactions, and the higher the rate of tax the stronger the incentive to substitute in-kind transactions for monetary transactions. Moreover, the higher the rate of tax, the greater the return from investing in seeking privileged tax treatment relative to the return from investing in socially productive activities. Billions of dollars are spent annually in trying to evade taxes, avoid taxes, seek out nontaxable forms of income, and secure privileged tax treatment. The amount of

---

[12] See, for instance, Friedrich A. Hayek, *The Constitution of Liberty* (Chicago: University of Chicago Press, 1959), p. 91.

this excess burden, which is largely generated by the highly progressive structure of nominal rates of tax, could itself promote a substantial war on poverty.

There seems little question but that a genuine consensus exists to the effect that the primary distributional concern of our fiscal system should be to assist the unfortunate, not to penalize the fortunate. A game in which people have a chance to win above average incomes necessarily requires that they may win below average incomes. But the primary topic of concern is not the inequality of rewards, but that the game is fair and that the lowest returns attain some minimum level. Fair treatment ex ante, however, is compatible with unequal returns ex post. A tax system designed to promote equality of opportunity rather than to penalize the wealthy would differ considerably from our present system. Progression in tax rates would be reduced substantially, if not eliminated altogether. The highly progressive portions of our tax system raise little revenue and are counterproductive in important respects, for they are incapable of providing greater opportunity to disadvantaged citizens to earn higher incomes and to amass greater wealth. Below some minimal level of income, a strong case exists for implementing some such program for income maintenance as a wage subsidy or a negative income tax. Such a combination of treating wealth transfers as income, taxing income at proportionate rates, and providing for income maintenance, seems far more capable of making a positive contribution to the equalization of opportunity than the prevailing punitive system of highly progressive nominal rates of tax on wealth transfers and income.

APPENDIX
Transfer Taxation in the United States

Since an analysis of our system of transfer taxation must be informed by a knowledge of the salient features of the system, the essential features of this system are described in this appendix. Since I want only to present the broad outlines of our transfer tax system, I necessarily ignore or oversimplify many of the complexities of tax administration.

Federal Estate Taxation

A decedent's estate tax liability is determined by following a four-step procedure. First, the value of the *gross estate* is estimated. Second, various exemptions and deductions are subtracted to determine the value of the *taxable estate*. Third, the *gross estate tax* is computed from the tax rate schedule shown in Table A-1. Fourth, the *net estate tax payable* is calculated by subtracting from the gross estate tax certain credits against the tax.

Gross estate.[1] The estimation of a decedent's gross estate is simple in principle but complex in practice. The valuation of real estate for local property taxation is fraught with well-known complexities, and the problems of assessing the gross estate are similar to those of assessing local real estate, except that real estate is only a small portion of the property covered by the estate tax. The gross estate of a decedent is estimated by making an inventory valuation of all the decedent's property, real and personal, tangible and intangible. As Table A-2 shows, corporate stock, real estate, and cash comprised

[1] The definition and valuation of gross estate is covered in Sections 2031-2044 of the Internal Revenue Code of 1954.

Table A-1

FEDERAL ESTATE TAX SCHEDULE

Taxable Estate		Gross Estate Tax	
At least: but	less than:	Base plus percent of excess over:	
$ 0	$ 5,000	3%	$ 0
5,000	10,000	$ 150 + 7%	5,000
10,000	20,000	500 + 11%	10,000
20,000	30,000	1,600 + 14%	20,000
30,000	40,000	3,000 + 18%	30,000
40,000	50,000	4,800 + 22%	40,000
50,000	60,000	7,000 + 25%	50,000
60,000	100,000	9,500 + 28%	60,000
100,000	250,000	20,700 + 30%	100,000
250,000	500,000	65,000 + 32%	250,000
500,000	750,000	145,700 + 35%	500,000
750,000	1,000,000	233,200 + 37%	750,000
1,000,000	1,250,000	325,700 + 39%	1,000,000
1,250,000	1,500,000	423,200 + 42%	1,250,000
1,500,000	2,000,000	528,200 + 45%	1,500,000
2,000,000	2,500,000	753,200 + 49%	2,000,000
2,500,000	3,000,000	998,200 + 53%	2,500,000
3,000,000	3,500,000	1,263,200 + 56%	3,000,000
3,500,000	4,000,000	1,543,200 + 59%	3,500,000
4,000,000	5,000,000	1,838,200 + 63%	4,000,000
5,000,000	6,000,000	2,468,200 + 67%	5,000,000
6,000,000	7,000,000	3,138,200 + 70%	6,000,000
7,000,000	8,000,000	3,838,200 + 73%	7,000,000
8,000,000	10,000,000	4,568,200 + 76%	8,000,000
10,000,000 and over		6,088,200 + 77%	10,000,000

Source: Internal Revenue Code of 1954, Section 2001.

over 60 percent of gross estates in 1965. Although the gross estate is normally valued as of the date of death, the executor may elect to have the estate valued as of either the date of sale of property in the estate or one year after the decedent's death.

Taxable estate.[2] Several deductions and exemptions are subtracted from the gross estate to determine the taxable estate. Every estate is allowed to take a specific exemption of $60,000. Deductions are allowed for funeral expenses and the expenses of administering the estate, as well as for the decedent's unpaid debts and taxes. Bequests to approved, tax-exempt, charitable, educational, or religious institutions are also deductible from the gross estate. If the decedent is

[2] The deductions and exemptions from the gross estate that yield the taxable estate are covered in Sections 2051-2056 of the Internal Revenue Code of 1954.

Table A-2

GROSS ESTATE, DEDUCTIONS, AND ESTATE TAX, 1965

($ in millions)

Gross estate:			
Corporate stock		$ 9,215	
Real estate		4,275	
Cash		2,612	
Bonds		1,491	
Trust and remainder interests		1,345	
Life insurance		1,112	
Notes and mortgages		720	
Noncorporate business assets		549	
Household goods and other assets		344	
Annuities		95	
Total gross estate			$21,757
Deductions:			
Specific exemption	$5,339		
Marital deduction	4,090		
Charitable bequests	1,309		
Debts	1,112		
Administrative expenses	795		
Funeral expenses	150	$12,795	
Less: lifetime transfers		198	
Total deductions			$12,598
Taxable estate:			$ 9,160
Gross estate tax:			$ 2,755
Less credits			
State death taxes	$ 280		
Foreign, gift, and prior estate taxes	61		
Total credits			$ 341
Net estate tax payable:			$ 2,412

Source: Internal Revenue Service, *Statistics of Income—1965, Fiduciary, Gift, and Estate Tax Returns* (Washington: U.S. Government Printing Office, 1967), p. 58.

survived by a spouse, a marital deduction of up to 50 percent of noncommunity property in the adjusted gross estate (which is the gross estate less deductions for expenses and debts) may be taken. An adjusted gross estate of $120,000, for instance, could be reduced to $60,000 by taking the full marital deduction. When the specific exemption is then applied, the taxable estate becomes zero.

Table A-2 shows that deductions totaled nearly $13 billion in 1965, which was about 60 percent of the gross estate value. The

Table A-3

FEDERAL CREDIT FOR STATE DEATH TAXES

Taxable Estate		Amount of Credit	
At least:	but less than:	Base plus percent of excess over:	
$ 40,000	$ 90,000	0.8%	$ 40,000
90,000	140,000	$ 400 + 1.6%	90,000
140,000	240,000	1,200 + 2.4%	140,000
240,000	440,000	3,600 + 3.2%	240,000
440,000	640,000	10,000 + 4.0%	440,000
640,000	840,000	18,000 + 4.8%	640,000
840,000	1,040,000	27,600 + 5.6%	840,000
1,040,000	1,540,000	38,800 + 6.4%	1,040,000
1,540,000	2,040,000	70,800 + 7.2%	1,540,000
2,040,000	2,540,000	106,800 + 8.0%	2,040,000
2,540,000	3,040,000	146,800 + 8.8%	2,540,000
3,040,000	3,540,000	190,800 + 9.6%	3,040,000
3,540,000	4,040,000	238,800 + 10.4%	3,540,000
4,040,000	5,040,000	290,800 + 11.2%	4,040,000
5,040,000	6,040,000	402,800 + 12.0%	5,040,000
6,040,000	7,040,000	522,800 + 12.8%	6,040,000
7,040,000	8,040,000	650,800 + 13.6%	7,040,000
8,040,000	9,040,000	786,800 + 14.4%	8,040,000
9,040,000	10,040,000	930,800 + 15.2%	9,040,000
10,040,000 and over		1,082,800 + 16.0%	10,040,000

Source: Internal Revenue Code of 1954, Section 2011.

specific exemption and the marital deduction accounted for over $5 billion and $4 billion, respectively. Expenses and debts accounted for just over $2 billion, and charitable bequests just over $1 billion.

Gross estate tax. Once the decedent's taxable estate is determined, the gross estate tax is determined as indicated by the tax rate schedule shown in Table A-1. The total amount of gross estate tax for 1965 was $2.7 billion, which was more than 30 percent of the value of taxable estates and was nearly 13 percent of the value of gross estates.

Net estate tax payable. Several credits are allowed against gross estate tax. The total value of such credits exceeded $0.3 billion for 1965, which reduced the net estate tax payable to $2.4 billion.

The most significant credit is the one allowed for state death tax payments, the rate schedule for which is shown in Table A-3.[3] Table A-1 shows that the gross estate tax on a taxable estate of

[3] The credits against gross estate tax are covered in Sections 2011-2016 of the Internal Revenue Code of 1954.

$1,000,000 is $325,700. Table A-3 shows that if a state levies a tax upon either the estate or its distribution, the amount of state death tax payments up to a maximum of $36,500 can be credited against gross estate tax. For instance, if the state levied death taxes of exactly $36,500, the net estate tax payable to the federal government would be reduced to $289,140.

Several less significant credits also exist. Credits may be allowed for death taxes paid to a foreign country. Credit is allowed for gift taxes paid by the decedent if the property upon which the gift tax was paid is subsequently included in the decedent's estate. Finally, credit is sometimes given for previous estate tax payments under what is referred to as the provision for quick succession relief. Suppose the husband predeceases the wife by, for example, one year. Without a provision for quick succession relief, the estate is taxed once upon the husband's death and again upon the wife's death. Quick succession relief softens the force of this double taxation of an estate. If the wife dies within two years of the husband, the wife's estate is given credit for 100 percent of her husband's estate tax payment. If the wife's death occurs within the third or fourth year following her husband's death, the credit is 80 percent of the husband's tax payment, and the credit continues to decline at 20 percent increments at each two-year interval until it vanishes once the wife survives the husband by ten years.

Federal Gift Taxation [4]

The federal gift tax is viewed as a complement to the federal estate tax, not as an independent tax. Gift taxation was instituted and is maintained primarily to increase the yield of the estate tax. In the absence of a gift tax, a prospective decedent could escape estate tax liability by transferring wealth before his death. By reducing this incentive to make inter vivos gifts, the gift tax works to increase the amount of wealth being transferred at death and subject to the estate tax.

The complementarity between the estate tax and the gift tax is shown by the nearly identical structures of the two taxes. As Table A-4 shows, the gift tax has the same rate and bracket structure as the estate tax; the only difference is that for each bracket the rate

[4] The determination of gift tax liability is covered in Sections 2501-2504 of the Internal Revenue Code of 1954. The definition and valuation of transfers subject to tax are covered in Sections 2511-2517; deductions and exemptions from the tax are covered in Sections 2521-2524.

Table A-4
FEDERAL GIFT TAX SCHEDULE

Taxable Gifts		Gift Tax Liability	
At least: but	less than:	Base plus percent of excess over:	
$ 0	$ 5,000	2¼ %	$ 0
5,000	10,000	$ 112.50 + 5¼ %	5,000
10,000	20,000	375.00 + 8¼ %	10,000
20,000	30,000	1,200.00 + 10½ %	20,000
30,000	40,000	2,250.00 + 13½ %	30,000
40,000	50,000	3,600.00 + 16½ %	40,000
50,000	60,000	5,250.00 + 18¾ %	50,000
60,000	100,000	7,125.00 + 21 %	60,000
100,000	250,000	15,525.00 + 22½ %	100,000
250,000	500,000	49,275.00 + 24 %	250,000
500,000	750,000	109,275.00 + 26¼ %	500,000
750,000	1,000,000	174,900.00 + 27¾ %	750,000
1,000,000	1,250,000	244,275.00 + 29¼ %	1,000,000
1,250,000	1,500,000	317,400.00 + 31½ %	1,250,000
1,500,000	2,000,000	396,150.00 + 33¾ %	1,500,000
2,000,000	2,500,000	564,900.00 + 36¾ %	2,000,000
2,500,000	3,000,000	748,650.00 + 39¾ %	2,500,000
3,000,000	3,500,000	947,400.00 + 42 %	3,000,000
3,500,000	4,000,000	1,157,400.00 + 44¼ %	3,500,000
4,000,000	5,000,000	1,378,650.00 + 47¼ %	4,000,000
5,000,000	6,000,000	1,851,150.00 + 50¼ %	5,000,000
6,000,000	7,000,000	2,353,650.00 + 52½ %	6,000,000
7,000,000	8,000,000	2,878,650.00 + 54¾ %	7,000,000
8,000,000	10,000,000	3,426,150.00 + 57 %	8,000,000
10,000,000 and over		4,566,150.00 + 57¾ %	10,000,000

Source: Internal Revenue Code of 1954, Section 2502.

of gift tax is set at three-quarters of the rate of estate tax. The gift tax follows the same format for determining tax liability as the estate tax: A valuation is first placed upon the gifts made by the donor, certain exemptions and deductions are then taken to determine the value of taxable gifts, and the gift tax liability is finally computed. Since the gift tax is governed by the same essential principles as the estate tax, we shall describe only those features of the gift tax that are not found in the estate tax.

Liability for gift tax is cumulative over a donor's lifetime at the rates given in Table A-4. For each year that a donor makes taxable gifts, his tax liability for that year is computed as the difference between his cumulated lifetime tax liability and his previous gift tax payments. To illustrate, consider an individual who as of one year ago had made lifetime taxable gifts of $80,000, upon which his gift tax payments were $11,325. During the current year suppose he makes additional taxable gifts of $40,000. His cumulated value of taxable gifts has risen to $120,000, upon which the gift tax is $20,025. Given his previous payments of $11,325, his additional tax liability for the current year would be $8,700.

The gift tax provides two forms of exemption—a specific lifetime exemption of $30,000 and an annual per donee exemption of $3,000. A donor may give up to $3,000 per year free of tax, with no limit on either the number of years or the number of donees. Gifts, then, enter the tax base only to the extent that a donee receives more than $3,000 in any one year. To illustrate the impact of the annual exemption, consider three donors, each of whom makes gifts of $30,000 during the year and has previously exhausted his $30,000 specific exemption. Let the first make a single gift of $30,000, the second three gifts of $10,000 each, and the third ten gifts of $3,000 each. After subtracting the annual per donee exemption, the value of taxable gifts would be $27,000 for the first donor, $21,000 for the second donor, and zero for the third.

Both the actual tax rates and the annual per donee exemption feature serve to make the effective tax rate on gifts lower than that on estates. The rate of tax on gifts is further lowered relative to that on estates by the exemption of gift tax payments from the base of the gift tax. If a donor makes a taxable gift of $60,000, the donee receives $60,000 and the donor pays a gift tax of $7,125. The total amount of wealth transferred by the donor is $67,125—$60,000 to the donee and $7,125 to the Internal Revenue Service. If the gift tax base was determined in the same manner as the estate tax base, however, the amount of taxable gift would be $67,125. And with this size of taxable gift, the amount of gift tax would be $8,621.25, which would leave only $58,503.75 for the donee.

State Transfer Taxation

All states except Nevada impose death taxes; twelve use estate taxation and thirty-seven use inheritance taxation. Twelve states, moreover, levy a gift tax. Table A-5 shows that considerable variation exists in the rate schedules of the twelve states that practice estate taxation. Ohio provides a specific exemption of only $5,000, while Arizona provides one of $100,000. South Carolina has a nearly proportional tax rate, as the marginal tax rate is 4 percent on the first $40,000 of taxable estate and rises to 6 percent on the value in excess of $100,000. North Dakota, by contrast, has a steeply progressive estate tax, rising from 2 percent on the first $25,000 to 23 percent on the amount of taxable estate in excess of $1,500,000.

Table A-5

STATE ESTATE TAX RATES

State	Marginal Rate Range (on taxable estate)	Minimum Rate Applies To:	Maximum Rate Applies Above:	Specific Exemption
Alabama		Maximum federal credit		$ 60,000
Arizona	0.8%—16%	$50,000	$10,000,000	$100,000
Arkansas		Maximum federal credit		$ 60,000
Florida		Maximum federal credit		$ 60,000
Georgia		Maximum federal credit		$ 60,000
Mississippi	1%—16%	$60,000	$10,000,000	$ 60,000
New York	2%—21%	$50,000	$10,000,000	Variable
North Dakota	2%—23%	$25,000	$ 1,500,000	$ 20,000
Ohio	2%— 7%	$40,000	$ 500,000	$ 5,000
Oklahoma	1%—10%	$10,000	$10,000,000	$ 15,000
South Dakota	4%— 6%	$40,000	$ 100,000	$ 60,000
Utah	3%—10%	$10,000	$ 125,000	$ 10,000

Source: *Facts and Figures on Government Finance,* 15th ed. (New York: Tax Foundation, Inc., 1969), p. 200.

It should be noted that Alabama, Arkansas, Florida, and Georgia all duplicate the exemption and bracket structure of the federal estate tax, with their rates set equal to the maximum federal credit allowed on any given estate. If a decedent in one of these states left an estate of $1,040,000, the state would claim an estate tax of $38,800, which is the full value of the federal credit as shown in Table A-3. Five of the remaining eight states impose pickup taxes to ensure full absorption of the federal credit. Of the three remaining states, the tax liability in two (Mississippi and North Dakota) would clearly exceed the amount of maximum federal credit, leaving only one state (Utah) that may in some instances fail to take full advantage of the federal credit.

Table A-6 shows that considerable variation also exists in the rate schedules of the thirty-seven states that practice inheritance taxation. In New Jersey the rate of tax on transfers to spouse, child, or parent ranges from 1 to 16 percent, while in Delaware it ranges from 1 to 4 percent. The rate of tax on transfers to nonrelatives ranges from 8 to 40 percent in Wisconsin, while in Michigan it ranges from 10 to 15 percent. A similar degree of variation also exists in the size of the specific exemption. Kansas, for instance, permits a specific exemption of $75,000 on transfers to the surviving spouse, while Maryland allows only $150.

Although considerable variety exists in particular rate schedules, the primary features of the inheritance tax are quite similar among the states. All states except Oregon, for instance, vary the rate of tax with consanguinity, with the rate of tax declining as the transferee's relation to the transferor becomes closer. Maine, for instance, taxes transfers to spouse, child, or parent at 2 to 6 percent, transfers to brother or sister at 8 to 12 percent, and transfers to nonrelatives at 12 to 18 percent. All states except Oregon and Maryland, moreover, vary the size of the specific exemption directly with the degree of consanguinity.

Except for Oregon, South Dakota, and West Virginia, states that use an inheritance tax also impose a pickup tax upon the estate in the event the inheritance tax collected from the shares of the estate is too small to absorb the full amount of the federal credit. A federal taxable estate of $240,000, for instance, is allowed a maximum credit of $3,600 for state death tax payments. If a state collects only $2,600 in inheritance taxes from the distribution of the estate, the state would levy a pickup tax of $1,000 against the estate in order to absorb fully the federal credit.

Table A-6
STATE INHERITANCE TAX RATES AND EXEMPTIONS

State	Marginal Rate Range (in percent)			Exemptions ($ thousands)			
	Spouse, Child or Parent	Brother or sister	Other than relative	Spouse	Child or parent	Brother or sister	Other than relative
Alaska	1 - 3.5	3-10-5	5-17.5	$ 10	$ 10	$ 1	None
California	3 -14	6-20	10-24	5	5	2	0.3
Colorado	2 - 8	3-10	10-19	35	10	2	0.5
Connecticut	2 - 8	4-10	8-14	50	10	3	0.5
Delaware	1 - 4	2- 5	5- 8	20	3	1	None
Hawaii	2 - 7.5	3.5- 9	3.5- 9	20	5	0.5	0.5
Idaho	2 -15	4-20	8-20	10	4	1	None
Illinois	2 -14	2-14	10-30	20	20	10	0.1
Indiana	1 -10	5-15	7-20	15	2	0.5	0.1
Iowa	1 - 8	5-10	10-15	40	10	None	None
Kansas	0.5 - 5	3-12.5	10-15	75	15	5	0.2
Kentucky	2 -10	4-16	6-16	10	5	1	0.5
Louisiana	2 - 3	5- 7	5-10	5	5	1	0.5
Maine	2 - 6	8-12	12-18	15	10	0.5	0.5
Maryland	1	7- 5	7- 5	0.15	0.15	0.15	0.15
Massachusetts	1.25-11.25	5-18.75	7.5-18.75	10	10	1	1

Michigan	2 - 8	2- 8	10-15	30	5	5	None
Minnesota	1 - 5-10	6-25	8-30	30	6	1.5	0.5
Missouri	1 - 6	3-18	5-30	20	5	0.5	0.1
Montana	2 - 8	4-16	8-32	20	2	0.5	None
Nebraska	1	1	6-18	10	10	10	0.5
New Hampshire	Exempt	10	10	Unlimited	Unlimited	None	None
New Jersey	1 -16	11-16	15-16	5	5	0.5	0.5
New Mexico	1	5	5	Follows Variable Formula			
North Carolina	1 -12	4-16	8-17	10	2	None	None
Oregon	1 -10	1-10	1-10	None	None	1	0.5
Pennsylvania	6	15	15	1	None	None	None
Rhode Island	2 - 9	3-10	8-15	10	10	5	1
South Dakota	1 - 8	3-12	5-20	15	3	0.5	0.1
Tennessee	1.04- 9.5	6.5-20	6.5-20	Follows Variable Formula			
Texas	1 - 6	3-10	5-20	25	25	10	0.5
Vermont	2 - 6	3- 6	12	15	15	15	None
Virginia	1 - 5	2-10	5-15	5	5	2	1
Washington	1 -10	3-20	10-25	10	10	1	None
West Virginia	3 -13	4-18	10-30	15	5	None	None
Wisconsin	2 -10	2-10	8-40	15	2	0.5	0.1
Wyoming	2	2	6	10	10	10	None

Source: *Facts and Figures on Government Finance,* 15th ed. (New York: Tax Foundation, Inc., 1969), pp. 198-99.

Book and cover design: Pat Taylor